CRUSHING IT
IN COLLEGE

Your **7-Step** Guide to an
Awesome Adventure

CRUSHING IT IN COLLEGE

Your **7-Step** Guide to an
Awesome Adventure

ALICIA J. MOORE

ISBN: 9798987741832
(epub)
(AMA)
(Kindle)
(Audio)
(Apple Books)
(Ingram Spark)

Library of Congress Control Number: 2023902032

READER'S BONUS:

Thank you for purchasing this book! As a special bonus, if you would like to receive a PDF of "Crushing it in College: Your Pre-College Checklist to an Awesome Adventure," please visit the author's website at www.aliciajmoore.com, and sign up to receive one.

Contents

INTRODUCTION

Y ou've put in all the work to get to this point. You've done all the research on which colleges to apply to, the essay writing, test taking, GPA getting, interviewing...Now, at long last, you've been accepted—HOORAY—and will be heading off to college in the fall.

This may be the first time you are leaving home, leaving your family and community and friends behind. Along with anticipation, you feel the pressure start to build.

- Are ready to strike out on your own and can't wait to begin? Or are you feeling a little hesitant, or even a lot nervous, about taking that first step?

- Have you been dreaming about this all your life? Or have you barely thought about college—other than as the expected "next step?"

- Are you the first one in your family to go to college? Or is there a campus building at your college named after one of your ancestors?

- Do you think that college will be the best time in your life—the parties, the pranks, the all-nighters, the best friends for life— and you are so ready for that? Or have you heard the cautionary tales of out-of-control drinking, hazing, drug use, dropouts, and more, and think maybe you're not quite ready for that?

Maybe you've asked yourself: Will I fit in? Can I make the grades? How will I know what classes to pick? How will I pick my major? What if I don't get along with my roommate? What if... So many unknowns!

Whether you plan to attend a junior college, a community college, or a four-year college or university, heading off to college for the first time can be a little like traveling to a foreign country where you don't speak the language and don't have a map. You know that you are going to have new challenges and you wonder whether you will be able to meet them.

You ask yourself: Will the learning curve be too steep? Am I really equipped for this adventure? Am I really ready for this?!

There are tons of books about how to choose and get into college, but very few to help you prepare yourself to succeed once you're there. This is the one you need now that you've gotten in.

Throughout my career, I have helped hundreds of individuals, teams, and companies explore, set, and successfully achieve their goals. As a member of the Board of Directors for the innovative Bay Area Resource Area for Teachers (RAFT), an educational nonprofit that supports teachers and promotes STEAM and kinesthetic learning, I've continued my passion to help people reach their potential. With degrees from Stanford and UCLA School of Law, and post-graduate certificates from Stanford and UC Berkeley's Haas School of Business, I learned how to crush it in college. I have seen students both flourish and flounder, and have observed some patterns that successful students have in common. I've written this guide to help you achieve success, too!

Using composite anecdotes, practical tips, personal challenges, and proven strategies, this guide delves into seven steps you can take to set yourself up for success in college and beyond. If you follow the steps, you will:

- *Clarify your personal mission, goals, and motivations, so you can make this journey your own and move forward with momentum (Chapter 1).*

- *Identify your personal strengths and advantages, and make mindset choices so you can fuel your success and propel your progress (Chapter 2).*

- *Plot your journey and choose your courses, even if you don't know your major, so you can create your unique map to reach your goals (Chapter 3).*

- *Gain tips on how to orient yourself to your new environment and set yourself up for success at the outset (Chapter 4).*

- *Add tools to find your people and strengthen your social life (Chapter 5).*

- *Create effective study habits and time management, so you can reach your goals with less stress (Chapter 6).*

- *Secure strategies for recovering from setbacks, so you can overcome obstacles and missteps that arise along the way and keep making forward progress (Chapter 7).*

From discovering your unique personal mission to inspire you, to clearly defining your goals and creating your unique plan to accomplish them, this guide provides a framework for making decisions, a resource to count on for support, and proven strategies and practical suggestions that have helped many students not just to survive, but to thrive, in college. The seven simple steps have worked for them and can work for you, too!

A word of warning, however. Just as you can't build muscles merely by reading about pushups, to get results you actually have to dig in and do the work! Decide up front actively to engage in the challenges in each chapter, rather than just skimming through. Invest time and effort to build your roadmap to success. You'll feel more confident and be more prepared for your college experience if you do.

Once you have read this book and done the work, you will be prepared to take on this incredible journey and the obstacles you'll face. You'll have created your own personalized roadmap to make your college experience the best it can be. You're in for an awesome adventure!

Chapter 1

UNPACK BEFORE YOU PACK

"There are two important days in your life: the day
you were born, and the day you find out why."

—Mark Twain

Pete was SO excited to start college, and it seemed like everyone else in his dorm was too—even the people who were trying really hard to look cool. It was the first day in his all-freshman, co-ed dorm. Everyone was hauling in clothes and bedding and lamps and fans and room organizers, and more, and excitedly meeting and greeting their dormmates and RAs.

All except for Pete's roommate, Rex, who was a no-show. And not just for the first day, but for the entire first week! Rex missed the freshman welcome lecture and the get-to-know-you socials. He missed the club sign-up days. He missed the campus orientation tours, the department tours, and the pre-semester parties the week before class.

This was definitely not standard behavior at his uber-competitive university. The mysterious Rex became a hot topic of conversation, inspiring jokes and creative conspiracy theories. The people on Pete's floor in the dorm, where Rex was supposed to reside, had taken to planting a crown (for "Rex the King") around campus. They arranged a dorm-wide scavenger hunt to find the crown, with extra points if you could find the actual Rex, who, at this point, still had not been spotted. Even the RA was stumped. Where was Rex?

When Rex missed the first few days of class, Pete began celebrating that he wouldn't have to share a room with anyone. Then who shows up? Rex, of course. With just a backpack and an engaging grin, he explained that he'd been traveling and wasn't completely sure when classes started. Rex said his dad was a doctor, and that Rex had pre-registered for a pre-med major. But Rex said he wasn't sure he even liked science. He still hadn't decided on which classes he would take this semester.

Perhaps most shocking—especially to those like Pete who had worked so hard for so many years just to have the opportunity to be accepted to this university—Rex said he wasn't entirely certain that he wanted to be there.

Rex signed up for classes that were still open at that late date, but with no great enthusiasm. He attended some of his classes, but mostly slept in. He was friendly, but generally didn't participate in any activities.

Rex was super smart, as anyone who had a conversation with him could tell. But he didn't seem to have any goals, or purpose, or plan. He didn't have any clear idea about why he was even there, other than that it was "expected of him" and this seemed to be the "next step." In the end, no one was really surprised when Rex dropped out after his first set of mid-terms.

If you don't know WHERE you're going, how will you know if you get there? And if you don't know WHY you're going, will YOU really care?

You should be excited, and maybe nervous, about taking this journey. Attending college is a big step away from the people, places, and systems that you have grown up with. A step away from the familiar you that you currently are and the first step toward the you that you will become. But do you know why you want to embark on this adventure? Are you clear on what you hope to achieve by your journey's end?

Some people go to college just because it seems to be "the next step." Some go on athletic scholarships with the intent to showcase their talents and be scouted to the Pros, with no particular interest in the courses offered. Some people are actively seeking a way to improve their future financial prospects. Some want to learn a trade. Some people are using college to hide out from the "real world" for a bit. For some, it is a necessary step towards a graduate degree in law, medicine, or business. Do you know your reason? And how important is it to you?

Going to college is expensive in both time and money, and it will challenge you in ways that you haven't been challenged before. It will stretch your thinking and push you to the edge of your capabilities, determination, and self-beliefs. So to make sure that you get the most out of this journey, it is essential that you take some time and thought to ***unpack* your reasons for going *before you pack* to go**.

In this chapter, you will begin to uncover your core motivation to undertake this adventure, define your unique mission, and articulate the goals you want to achieve from your college adventure.

 **SET YOUR COMPASS:**
FIND YOUR TRUE NORTH

To some extent, all the time and effort that you've spent working up to this moment has been in preparation for this adventure. But ask yourself: Is this *your* plan? Or have you simply been following the courses and paths that have been set out for you? This is the first step of the rest of your life. It's important to know that it's yours; and to put in the energy to make it yours.

It's trite but true: **If you don't know where you are going, you are unlikely to get there.** You certainly won't get there in the fastest, easiest way. Unpacking your mission, your unique purpose, is a key first step in moving toward your future success.

One major difference between college and high school is that **YOU** will have lots and lots of opportunities to **CHOOSE**. Well beyond the electives you may have had in high school, in college you will have the chance to make (and sometimes change) decisions about your classes, your major, your social activities, how you spend your time and money, how much effort you expend, and what you learn.

Maybe for the first time ever, **you** will be in charge of your journey. You will decide where you will go and how you will get there. Decide up front: **Are you going to be the pilot or a passenger on this trip?** Are you ready to maximize your forward momentum? Or are you just marking time?

You can choose simply to drift downstream (and maybe run adrift) taking minimal classes toward graduation. Doing the minimum necessary to get by, gliding with the tide. Or you can choose to take hold of the paddle, set your own course, and gain the knowledge and experiences that will propel you into the life *you* design. It is *your* choice.

The culmination of your choices, large and small, will define your journey. Whether or not you know where you're going, you will get somewhere sometime. Now is the time to think about how you can get the most out of your adventure. So how can you increase your chances of ending up where you'd like to be?

It starts with **GOALS**.

AVOID UNNECESSARY TOLLS BY SETTING GOALS

Almost everyone who is successful sets goals. Whether they shout them out to the world or keep them privately to themselves, successful people almost always have them. And you can too. You can decide to keep them to yourself, or you can announce them out loud (especially if that strengthens them for you and helps keep you accountable). Either way, having goals is the difference between floating through life and making things happen. It is the difference between missing opportunities and seeing the possibilities to make your dreams a reality.

In his book *Seven Habits of Highly Effective People*, Stephen Covey says to "Begin with the end in mind." If you know where you are going before you head out, you can avoid a lot of unnecessary U-turns. You can allocate resources, time, and energy to the pursuits that best serve you. You can create a roadmap to your destination and build a system for tracking your progress.

So how do you do this? Start by thinking about **what you want**. Most people can rattle off a huge list of what they *don't* want, but at best only have a vague idea of what they *do* want. Flip that script!

Know What You Want

This is *your* life. Maybe for the first time, *you* will be the one directing the path. It is essential to be clear about what you want, your goals and destination, in order to achieve it. Knowing yourself on a deeper level, knowing where you want to go and what you want to accomplish, will guide you to your destination. By defining your destination, you give yourself a target to aim toward, and a means of checking whether you are on track to achieving what you want to achieve.

But what if you don't have goals? What if even the idea of setting goals is intimidating? Or what if you are afraid of setting goals because you're afraid you won't achieve them? What if you just don't know how to do it?!!

CHALLENGE #1: GATHER YOUR GOALS

What do you want from this adventure? Think about all of the aspects of your college journey: academic, social, emotional, physical, spiritual. Include every dimension that means something to you. Give yourself some time to brainstorm and really take stock of all of the things you'd like to learn, develop, and achieve. Write down on paper, in a journal, on your computer, or even in notes on your cellphone, all of the things that you'd ideally like to gain from your college experience. Write down anything and everything, without editing or second-guessing yourself.

Cast a broad net, but at the same time, be as specific as you can. Maybe you'd like to gain a specific number of friends and build a focused network, or achieve a certain GPA. Maybe you'd like to take leadership role in a campus club (or several), or join a particular fraternity or sorority. Maybe you'd like to achieve a certain record in a sport. Or play a musical instrument in a jazz band on or off campus. Maybe you'd like to gain particular skills that you can identify, or want to receive acceptances to certain graduate schools, or have a specific number of job offers, or a particular type of job offer by graduation...

Anything and everything that you'd personally like to achieve should go on this list. Big dreams and small wins. The sky's the limit.

If you are attending a community college, think about the schools to which you'd like to transfer, but don't stop there. Is there a GPA you'd like to achieve? Certain skills you'd like to gain? Take your imagination all the way through graduation, with a degree in hand, and all of the accomplishments you'd like to achieve throughout your journey.

Once you define for yourself what you want from your college experience, you will be able to winnow your choices to help you target your goals. When considered against your goals, your future decisions—like what classes to take, how to spend your free time, how much effort to make on any given project, which clubs to join—all will become easier.

But What if You Don't Know What You Want?

Sometimes people don't know what they want when they start out. They've been pressured to find their passion, but it hasn't worked. They are good at a lot of things, but not drawn to any one thing. And the thought of picking a major stresses them out. So what to do if this is you?

Survey the Landscape and Consider Your Options

If you truly don't know what you want, begin by taking a look at what your college has to offer. Peruse the majors and examine the course offerings. See if any call out to you, and if many do, think about what specifically makes them interesting to you. What do those majors have in common? Do they revolve around research, communication, thinking deep philosophical thoughts? Even if no major evokes a particular passion, you should be able to find at least one that resonates with you on some level. Choose one and use it as your baseline.

Play to Your Strengths, and Strengthen Them

Although you are not required to continue to pursue those things you've excelled at in the past, your history may give some clues to guide your future journey. Just because you are good at something doesn't mean you have to continue to do it. However, the fact that you have experience and success in the past means that you have built up some skills. These skills can form a strong foundation on which you can build, if you choose to.

Think about subjects that have been easy for you and then ask yourself why they were easy. Is it because you read and synthesize material well? Write and communicate well? You're intrigued by solving problems? Enjoy logic?

If you don't have a burning passion for a particular major, use your affinities to plot a preliminary path. When you think about your future path, think about how to capitalize on your past skills and interests, and which potential majors will let you incorporate them. For example, your skills in logic can be used in math, pre-law, computer science or graphic design, or even art or philosophy. Think broadly about how you can shape what you like to do into your course choices.

Struggling with this? Make an appointment with your guidance counselor to discuss it. Set a goal to explore your options to find a passion, play to your strengths, or enhance generally marketable skills.

Nothing Lasts Forever

Sometimes people get stuck because they think that picking a major, or even beginning down a certain path, will bind them forever. Not true! Plans change, the world changes, and you will change. Your goals may change over time as you progress and grow. If you start out with your goals clearly in mind, you can (and should) periodically assess whether they still suit you. If they don't, you can adjust your path. But having a clear direction at the outset will keep you from wandering aimlessly and will give you markers to guide and assess your progress.

Holistic Goals for the Whole You

Make sure to include social, emotional, and physical goals in your planning. Think about the elements you personally need to maintain the health of your whole self. Spirituality or charitable service, if that is important to you. Or nutrition if you are committed to eating vegan, for example. Political involvement, if that matters to you. Or training for a marathon. Or building your social network. Try to incorporate all of the facets of life that are important to you in setting your preliminary goals.

These goals will be your baseline for discovering your personal true north: Always have a clear idea of where you are and where you want to be in the future—even if it changes over the years. Go back and do a written re-set as your goals evolve throughout your college journey, so that you can always have the bigger picture to guide your path and future decision-making.

It may take a little practice, but you can do this. And you'll see that once you've set your goals, they are powerful motivators!

So what do you REALLY want?

FUEL YOUR MOTIVATIONAL MOTOR

The WHY-O-U is all about YOU. Getting through college can be, and at times almost certainly will be, HARD. You will be challenged as you grow into the person you wish to become. Understanding the personal reasons **WHY** you are taking this journey is the secret sauce to keep you moving forward. Your "why" is your motivational motor oil; it keeps your mental, physical and spiritual engine running. Even if you change paths, or are blown off course, your "why" will enable you to find another way to accomplish your goals.

Once You've Identified WHAT You Want, It is CRITICAL to Know WHY You Want It

Many people who get into college know *what* they do (or at least have done so far) and *how* they do it (or at least how they have done it so far), but not *why* they are doing it—other than perhaps to get into college.

In the challenge above, you set out your goals, but this alone isn't always sufficient to get you through. **If you understand your personal reasons "why" you want to go to college, you can build an unshakeable foundation for making the countless decisions your college journey will require.**

To do this, begin by identifying your deepest personal motivations. *Why* are you taking this journey? What is your personal mission and why does it matter to you?

Deeper Than the Destination: Make Your Journey Epic

Think about this: **YOU are the hero of your own story.** Through your decisions, choices and actions, YOU will write how it goes. Knowing yourself, knowing who you are and what makes you tick will help you write the tale.

Sir Edmund Hillary said he climbed Mount Everest "because it was there." But we know there must be much more to the story. Something inside him drove him to endure all the hardships necessary to accomplish this goal. This college adventure is your Everest. You, too, will need more than "because it was there" if you want to extract everything you can out of your journey.

Take the time to understand your underlying motivations as you choose your personal peak. Ask yourself "why" you want what you do. Your answers may surprise you, or they may reinforce what you already know about yourself. Your answers will give you a key understanding about what motivates and inspires you. Your answers will give you a yardstick against which to measure your future choices, and the strength to endure the obstacles you may face along the way. The "why" behind your quest is what helps you make it epic. It sets your mission.

So how do you find your "why"? You'll need patience, determination, and maybe a little courage to dig really deep.

Channel Your Inner Child

Have you ever been around a three-year-old child? Their favorite word seems to be "why?" And no matter what you answer, their next answer is usually "but, why?" again and again until you finally run out of patience and end with "because I said so" or "I don't know." Now you'll need to channel that inner child, because once you've identified each of the goals you really WANT, then you'll need to ask yourself WHY you want each of those goals. Not just once, but seven or so times for each one. Not just superficially, but deep in your heart and the core of your being.

Your "why" will help you identify additional skills that can benefit you in support of your deeper purpose. Your goals can, and maybe will, change as you grow into your college journey, but your personal "whys" likely will not. If you understand your "whys" at the outset, you'll be able to focus on what's really important to you and disregard activities that don't support your goals. You'll be able to adapt your plans, weather the storms, and end up with awesome experiences, skills, and adventures.

Once you really understand your "whys" and goals, and their respective value to you, you can begin to see and shape your college mission. Your mission will keep you motivated to go over, around, under, or through any obstacles you encounter along the way. It will help answer the question: Now that you are in college, what do you want to get out of it? Beyond the vague "getting a degree," you will have a solid foundation on which to build what you personally want to achieve.

 **Conduct Your Own Personal Excavation**

But what if you don't know why you are going to college, other than "because it is the next step?" That's when to do a little soul searching. Be clear with yourself about your personal reasons for showing up each day and doing the work it's going to take to graduate.

Take the time and think about the deep, personal reasons you want to reach the goals you set for yourself. For example:

- Why do I want to go to college? *Because it's the next thing after high school.*

- Why do I want to do the next thing after high school? *Because I want to get a high-paying job after I graduate... because I want a career in law and I need a degree... because I want to increase my chances of getting hired in my chosen field....*

Whatever it is for you, define your "why" at this level.

- Why do I want a high paying job/a career in law/to be hired in this chosen field? *Because someday I want to buy a house... because I want to heal people... because I want to win an Oscar... because I want to make the world a better place....*

Go DEEPER.

- Why do I want to make the world a better place? *Because when I grew up, a friend of mine was bullied, and I don't want anyone else to feel that pain... because when I was young, my happiest times were _____, and I want that for everyone... because I thrive when I'm connected with people... because I get inspiration from imagining possibilities...*

Keep going until you truly can't go any deeper... and then try one more level. The deeper you go, the better your result will be. Once you reach the very bottom of your motivation, you'll have your "why." Do this exercise for each of your goals, large and small.

Just carrying out this exercise will help you discover your own guiding principles and help you define for yourself what you want from your awesome adventure. It helps you set your mission. Now any time you are stuck on a decision—which classes to take, what major to declare, whether to take a semester abroad, whether to sign up for a club or event, whatever the decision may be—you will have something against which to weigh your decision. Always ask yourself: Will this decision move me toward achieving my mission? If the answer is yes, you know what to do. If the answer is no, you also know what to do.

If you don't already know what you want to declare as your major, and many people don't, understanding the "why" of your personal goals will help you choose the classes you want to try, while still building skills that support your goals. Over time, you may discover your passion, or at least find out what you like—and don't like—to do. The insights you gain can open doors to majors that you might not have considered before, reinforce your current choice, or even help you discover that the major you thought you wanted isn't really for you after all.

CHALLENGE #2: DISCOVER WHAT DRIVES YOU

For each of the goals you identified in the previous exercise, ask yourself, "Why do I want this?" Then answer, "Because…" But don't stop there! Consider your "because" answer and ask yourself "why?" again. And then again. Keep digging and don't stop, even—and especially once—the answers become more difficult. Challenge yourself to push beyond the obvious. If it becomes too tough, take some time away, maybe ten minutes, an hour, or even a day to let your subconscious percolate. Then come back to it. Try to get to the base level of what makes you personally want that goal.

For example, your "why" goes beyond "I want to be a biology major because I want to be a doctor." Perhaps, when you dig deeper, you find "I want to be a doctor because I want to help people." Then ask yourself, "Why do I want to help people?" Keep going until you feel confident that you have hit your deepest "because." And then go deeper.

This exercise will help you assess, or reinforce, your path. It can help you choose, become more confident about, or in some cases change, your major. In the example above, you may start out with the intent to become a doctor, but realize the motivation came from wanting to please other people or to achieve status or financial security. You may then decide that you no longer want that career path because, if you are truly honest with yourself, those are not things you really value. You may discover that you hate biology or another required aspect of that career. If you know that one of your core "whys" is to help people, you can explore other ways to do that. You may find that you love medical research, or prefer to help people through social work, politics, teaching, or in another way.

The point is to discover your essential principles, values and needs; what lights you up and matters most to you at your core.

Mind the Gap (Year)

Maybe after thinking through all of this, you still cannot find any deep motivation to attend college or identify clear goals that you want to achieve. Maybe you feel that you really aren't ready to commit the time, money, or energy to make the most of your college experience quite yet. At this point, you have a few choices: You can go ahead and hope to figure things out on the fly at your college, you can work part-time and take a few general education courses at a community college to make progress while you figure it out, or you may want to consider a gap year between high school and college.

If you decide to take a gap year, think about what you plan to do in that time and what experiences will benefit you best. What do you hope to learn, how do you hope to develop, and how will you grow your skills, thinking, confidence, etc.? How will you use that year to gain clarity on life goals, or gain additional life skills? How will you finance that gap year? Your parents may have some thoughts on the matter, so it's best if you can include them in your plans and thinking. Check with your college admission office to see whether they will hold your slot for the following year, and what deadlines they have for making such a decision.

Conclusion

Your college years will go by more quickly than you realize, so knowing your mission and goals and choosing your path is critical to your experience.

Your "why" helps you set your destination and defines the general direction you will begin to take to reach *your* goals. It will give meaning to the time, effort, and money that you are investing.

Understanding your motivations, your unique "whys," will also help give you the resolve to make it through the tough times ahead. Together, your goals and your "whys" will give you your own "true north" to guide you as you progress along your path.

Remember Rex? He wasn't sure what he wanted, and he didn't have his WHY to help him weather that uncertainty. Because of that, he missed out on a major opportunity to grow and explore.

Pete took Rex's example to heart. Although he hadn't come in with a plan, he immediately set aside time to evaluate his goals and motivations. He developed a clear understanding of his mission, his path and why he was on it. He used his preliminary plan to evaluate the opportunities that arose. He used it when he spoke with his academic advisors, and to help him decide on which electives to take to determine his major. Over the years, whenever the going got tough, he would go back to his plan and purpose and reinvigorate himself. There was no question in Pete's mind that he would graduate. He promised himself that he would gain as much value as possible as he could from his college journey. And, four years later, he did!

College isn't for everyone. It's expensive in time, money, and effort. So if you're going to go, why not make the most of it? Unpack and define your goals, understand your "whys," and prepare to grab hold of your future!

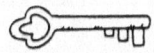 **KEY TIPS**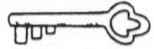

- THIS IS *YOUR* LIFE: MAKE A LIST OF YOUR GOALS (ACADEMIC, PHYSICAL, EMOTIONAL AND SOCIAL), AND WHAT SPECIFICALLY YOU'D LIKE TO GAIN FROM YOUR COLLEGE EXPERIENCE, TO SET THE DIRECTION OF YOUR JOURNEY.

- IF YOU DON'T KNOW WHAT YOU WANT TO DO, YOU CAN STILL MAKE VALUABLE PROGRESS BY UNDERSTANDING YOUR OPTIONS, WHAT THEY HAVE IN COMMON, AND BUILDING SKILLS THAT WILL HELP YOU SUCCEED REGARDLESS OF YOUR ULTIMATE DESTINATION.

- DEFINE THE DEEPEST MOTIVATION THAT UNDERLIES EACH OF YOUR GOALS, YOUR PERSONAL "WHY" FOR EACH ONE, TO FUEL YOUR MOMENTUM AND KEEP YOU ON TRACK.

Chapter 2

WHAT'S IN YOUR
DUFFEL BAG?

"You don't have to be great to start, but you DO have to start to be great."
—Zig Ziglar

By the time Maria was thirteen years old, she had moved eleven times. And not just across the street. Big moves: New York City, Florida, two other places in New York State, Colorado, Washington, D.C., a different place in Florida, Southern California, and Northern California. Because Maria's dad worked on projects that could take place anywhere in the U.S., they moved. A LOT. And often. Wrenching her away from people and places she had just come to know, disrupting relationships she was just starting to build.

This perpetual upheaval was maddening—not just the packing and unpacking and rearrangement of Maria's things, but having to start out again in new schools, constantly leaving friends and having to make new ones, trying to figure out the new social cues, constantly being the new kid, being so different from people who had kept familiar friends and customs their entire lives. It was pretty awful at times, always having to meet strangers, feeling out of step with people who had already formed their groups, worrying whether she'd be accepted or fit in.

And now, here she was, packing up to move into her college dorm, at her new college, in yet another new state. She shrugged her shoulders and stiffened her spine. "Once more into the breach," she thought. "It's not as if I've never done this before, and I've survived…"

Whether this will be your first time away from home, or whether you've traveled the world, whether you will be living on-campus or off-campus, with roommates or alone, you are about to embark on a journey that will include new experiences, challenges, and opportunities.

Before you pack your physical stuff, take a look at some of those psychological elements that you'll be packing as well, and decide what you want to take with you on your new adventure.

By breaking down your specific attributes, characteristics, and preferences, you can begin to collect what you have to work with (or work through or around) as you set out on your journey. By looking at these different pieces of you, knowing your strengths and weaknesses, you can give yourself an advantage marching into this new and unfamiliar territory.

 **SUMMON YOUR STRENGTHS**

You will be doing some heavy lifting in college: physical, mental, and emotional. You'll be hefting around your backpack crammed with your computer, water bottle, books, pens, glasses, and other paraphernalia.

You'll be listening hard, thinking hard, and doing heavy reading. You'll be dealing with new doubts, fears, challenges, and disappointments, and you'll be facing some difficult stuff that you'll need strength to overcome.

Think of it like this: Have you ever played a video game where your character gets to choose their weapons or superpowers? Or one where each of the characters is defined by their different capabilities?

Whether you realize it or not, you are the hero in your own journey. You already have a set of strengths, a unique combination of superpowers that you can pack for your journey. These strengths help form and inform your identity and provide a set of tools that you, like the characters in the video game, can call upon as you encounter new obstacles on your quest.

You have had life experiences that have formed who you are up until now. Values, beliefs, and lessons you've learned have all influenced how you've come to identify yourself. You've formed patterns in how you think, problem-solve, and process the world around you. You've had a chance to discover natural abilities and to hone your skills. These collective experiences, lessons, and abilities have become strengths that you already have in your toolkit to help you survive, and thrive, in college.

Assessing your strengths, and truly embracing the capabilities you already have, can help shape your view of yourself and give you a positive push when you need it. It can build your self-confidence and bolster your belief in yourself when your confidence is lagging. It can lend comfort when you suffer a setback, and give you the courage to strive to reach new heights. Having a list of your strengths in your back pocket, to remind you that "YES, I CAN," is an invaluable asset as you progress on your quest.

How Do You identify and Tap Into Your Strengths?

First, take inventory of yourself. Think about those things that always come easily for you. Natural skills and aptitudes. Think about characteristics for which you've received compliments from other people. Your quick wit. Your work ethic. Your sunny disposition. Your unflappable calm in a crisis. Your communication style.

Consider how, no matter how grim the situation, you can always make people laugh. Or how you take leadership of a group and set a direction. How you come up with new ideas and solutions. How you make connections quickly. How you can organize and plan anything that comes your way.

Maybe you're creative at coding. Maybe you're a great listener and have a knack for understanding material quickly. Maybe you're adept at understanding others. Maybe you're a genius at understanding math. Or maybe you have a gift for thinking deep thoughts and connecting deeper meanings. If you take the time and think about it, you can identify several strengths that you already have.

While you're at it, also think about those tough times that made you grow: those new skills that you had to develop, the fears you had to work to conquer, and the obstacles you had to overcome. Are you someone who bounces back from disappointments? Do you manage to push yourself forward even when you don't feel like it? How resilient are you? Or disciplined? Or brave? Have you ever had to work through a tragedy? What are some obstacles you've already overcome and how did you do it? Add these traits to your list of strengths. My guess is you're much stronger and wiser than you even know—and it's time you knew it too!

CHALLENGE #3: ASSEMBLE YOUR SKILLS

Before you head off on your journey, it's important to assess the tools you already have in your toolkit. Jot down those characteristics, values, and skills that comprise who you are and how you got here. Focus on your skills:

- What are you really good at? What comes naturally to you? Think about your passions, how you spend your free time, and what you most like to do. What have your friends, family, teachers, and others complimented you on? Are you organized? Flexible? Reliable? Creative? Clear in communicating? Talkative and engaging? Introspective? A good friend? List them all!

- Think about abilities and character traits that have helped you overcome obstacles. Are you good at getting back up and trying again after a setback? Good at learning from mistakes and growing from them? Do you try new things even when they're hard? Determined to find a way?

- Think about how you work best and achieve results. Can you tune in and focus despite distractions? Get into a deep thought zone in almost any environment? Quickly transition from one area to another? What makes you effective? Are you able to see the big picture? Focus on details? Are you able to synthesize information quickly? Are you good at selling your ideas?

- What role have you played effectively on a team? Motivating the group? Synthesizing ideas? Bringing people together? Organizing and delegating tasks? Communicating? Holding people accountable? Are you great at bringing out the best in your teammates? Focusing on your task and working hard? Are you dependable? Flexible? Supportive?

As you cast your mind over your life from the perspective of the skills you bring to the table, you'll be amazed at the capabilities you have already.

But wait, you may be thinking. I'm just an ordinary person and I have no idea what skills I've got. Can't I just skip this step and take it all as it comes? Here's the thing: Self-knowledge can be challenging, but the reward will be well worth the effort.

Knowing your strengths also provides a useful tool to guide you as you plan your journey. Reminding yourself of your strengths can bolster your confidence and remind you that you CAN do this. You can overcome obstacles that pop up on your journey and you can make it through to your chosen destination.

CHALLENGE #4: STEP INTO YOUR STRENGTHS.

Block out some time, say thirty minutes or so, and brainstorm all of your characteristics and tendencies that you can think of, large and small. The more you can come up with, the better. Once you have done that, think about what strengths each of them conveys. Note the ones that resonate best with you, that you feel represent you the best. Notice the ones that aren't as strong but are still part of your experiences. The collection of all of these strengths make you who you are.

If you're really feeling stuck, trying using this chart for some ideas to get you started:

Would you say . . .	Then your strength might be . . .
You are the person people can count on for a laugh or a joke no matter what's happening?	A great sense of humor, or an ability to change the mood of the room, or a quick wit
You are quiet, but people instinctively trust you?	Sensitivity, or trustworthiness, or wisdom

Would you say . . .	Then your strength might be . . .
You are a person who reads and is easily able to use and apply what you've just read?	Open-mindedness, or understanding, or connectivity
You are the one who gets the group going – plans an event or suggests an outing to the movies or another adventure?	Natural leadership
People confide in you a lot and turn to you when things are going hard for them?	Empathy, trustworthiness
You make friends easily wherever you go?	Super social skills
You don't get easily frustrated when plans change at the last minute?	Flexibility
You can defend your position, any position, to the death?	Determination
You can tune out anyone and anything when you're engaged in something?	Focus

You may not relate to any of the above examples, but they may help you find questions and answers that DO apply to you.

Remember that these strengths don't have to define you forever. Just because you are good at something, doesn't mean you have to continue to do it. But knowing that you have the skills and strengths to call on to tackle any challenge can be comforting indeed.

When you summon your strengths, you can find ways to problem-solve. You can find resilience in the face of challenges. You can retain confidence in trying times. By focusing on your strengths, you can also turn your experiences, good and bad, into valuable lessons that, in turn, will build more strengths.

And don't forget that you will gain new skills and strengths along the way. However, you have foundational support in your toolkit already as you're starting out. Anchor these strengths into your thoughts, keep them in your back pocket, and they will be there for you when times are tough (and you know sometimes they will be).

Your unique combination of skills and strengths are your superpowers that will help propel your success. Knowing your superpowers can be grounding and give you courage. You simply need to know what they are, that they are there for you, and intentionally bring them along as you embark on this adventure. Later, if you feel your confidence slipping, have doubts or hit obstacles, you can pull out your list of strengths and remember that you CAN do this!

 ## DUMP OUT THE DEADWEIGHT

Okay, let's be honest. Not all of us had the best high school experience, socially speaking. Maybe you ... :

- were shy.

- were a bit of a nerd in a school of jocks, or a jock in a school of nerds.

- stuttered.

- had braces.

- never had the right answer when called on in class.

- never felt that you could relate to your peers in a meaningful way.

- were bullied.

- were lonely.

- never felt that you fit in.

Regardless of what your high school experience was, here's the good news: Most colleges strive for a diverse student body. This means that you will have a much better chance there of finding like-minded and interesting people with whom to form friendships than you had in high school. College can be a fresh start and a new opportunity to define yourself in a new way. But it is up to you to grab the wheel and steer yourself to where you want to be.

You Can't Achieve if You Don't Believe

You may not be used to giving yourself permission to go for what you want. But you definitely have not only the permission, but the obligation, to make the most of your life. **You alone have the power to set goals for yourself, to work hard, and to achieve your dreams.** Whatever your background or history, you can take control of your journey. Allow yourself to believe, identify your goals, take action to achieve them, persist over obstacles, be flexible in your approach, and keep your eyes on your destination.

Your college's admissions office CHOSE YOU to be part of their incoming class. That means other people, whose job it is to bring in the strongest class they can, believe that you can succeed. They chose you because they think you will be an asset to their college. If you need to, borrow their belief until you believe it for yourself. Give yourself the courage to decide what you want, define the goals you'll need to get you there, and prove to yourself (and to them) that they were right!

Now you may be thinking: Look, thanks for the pep talk, but this all seems a bit much. I'm just like everybody else.

If that's what you are thinking, you are partially right: In some ways you ARE just like everybody else. Every college freshman is going through a similar transformation, at roughly the same time. You share many of the same worries, fears, inhibitions, and opportunities. The fact that you are surrounded by a group of people about the same age, going through a shared experience together, is one of the reasons that friends made in college often bond so deeply. Seize this extraordinary opportunity!

On the other hand, YOU are uniquely you. Your journey is a personal one—and that's where you'll find your unique secret sauce for success. Ask yourself: What are the specific elements of you that, taken as a whole, make up your unique self—both your strengths and the places where you have room to grow?

- Maybe you love to study, or maybe you hate to study.

- Maybe you can sit at the desk and focus hour after hour, or maybe you need to move to get your groove.

- Maybe you learn best in silence, or maybe you retain information best if you recite your notes out loud.

- Maybe you make outlines, or you prefer to do things on the fly.

- Maybe you are detail-oriented or maybe you see the big picture.

- Maybe you have a nearly photographic memory, or maybe you need to really work to retain information.

- Maybe you happily go to a party full of strangers, or maybe you would you rather do just about anything else.

Your success in college will strongly depend on how you view yourself and how you act. Your approach, attitude and actions all will make all the difference in whether you merely survive, or actually thrive, in college. The self-beliefs you bring and the actions you take (or don't take) are all on you now. If you are unhappy with yourself, a change of address won't change that. The good and bad news is that YOU are primarily in charge of your success.

Regret: Meet it, Greet it, and Leave it by the Side of the Road

You can't change the past, but you don't have to be imprisoned by it. College can be a clean slate: the present and future are yours to create. But just like the maxim that "the definition of insanity is doing the same thing over and over again and expecting a different result," you won't create a new result if you carry along the same old baggage of negative thoughts and doubts.

CHALLENGE #5: REFRAME YOUR REGRETS

Have you ever heard the saying "Confidence is silent; insecurities are loud"? We often take past mistakes and criticisms, and then tell ourselves that this is who we are, not just a mistake that we made. Maybe you misunderstood comments made to you, or maybe you were misunderstood by people who made those comments. It's time to clear out the rubbish and create a new narrative for your quest.

Block some time, say thirty minutes, and identify any self-doubts, limiting beliefs, fears, insecurities, or other negative baggage you are carrying. List as many of these as you can.

Next take a long look and see if you can find the root cause of these thoughts and why you think each is true. Is there a single incident that stands out in your mind? Or a group of incidents? Was it because of actions you took, or didn't take, that you formed your judgment?

Now let's test your opinion. See if you can create an argument to support why this isn't true all the time, or even at all.

I believe that I...	Because...	But this isn't always true, because...
Never have the right answers	I was called on in chemistry class junior year and I got the answer wrong in front of the whole class	I have other examples of when I was called on and got the answers right. For example...

I believe that I...	Because...	But this isn't always true, because...
Am terrible at public speaking	I am shy and stumble over words	I did give that great oral report to my history class and everyone commented on it afterward
Am horrible at math	My math teacher in fifth grade said I was stupid and can't do math	Although I needed extra tutoring from time to time, I got good scores on my college entrance math test
Am selfish	My friends in third grade said so when I wouldn't share my toys	I have grown since then, and I have been giving. For example...
Am no good	My Dad yelled at me for messing up his desk	I've done good things like the time when I [find your own examples]

The above examples may not apply to you, but they may spark ideas that DO. As you go through this challenge, you may be surprised to find that your view of yourself arose out of a single incident, or casual remark, made a long time ago that really has no relevance to who you are now. Use a fresh perspective to free yourself from bad baggage and replace your thoughts with those that will serve you.

Discover what is weighing you down and actively decide which of the negative stuff you are going to bring with you or, better yet, which you need to leave at home.

For example, maybe you didn't get into the college of your dreams. Maybe you didn't even get into your second or third choice. You will have a much better and more successful journey if you drop that disappointment and focus on making your experience the best that it can be. What you don't know now are the benefits that will come to you from being on this path. Maybe you will meet people that you may not have encountered otherwise. Maybe you will have a professor who ignites a lifelong passion. Maybe you will have opportunities to excel that you would not otherwise have had. Trust that you are where you should be and resolve to make the most of it.

Don't drive forward hung up on the view in the rearview mirror. Focus on your future and you won't miss the opportunities that await you down the road.

CHALLENGE #6: EMBRACE YOUR ADVANTAGES

In his book, *The Underdog Advantage: Rewrite Your Future by Turning Your Disadvantages into your Superpowers,* motivational speaker Dean Graziosi points out that many challenges and obstacles that have confronted you in the past can actually be a major advantage for you in the future. The underdog is the scrappy fighter who overcomes the odds to win. Many of us have some element of the underdog in us. If you've come from nothing, you've learned how to survive on little; you've become good at taking stock of and using the resources that you do have to full advantage. You've learned how not to waste resources and opportunities. If you've had to overcome other people doubting your abilities or goals, you've learned how to rely on your own vision to power you through. With tenacity, underdogs move through adversity. Underdogs find a way!

Think of the challenging experiences and disadvantages you've had to over-come, or negative things you've thought about yourself. You may be thinking of yourself as an underdog. Maybe you grew up in an economically disadvan-taged household. Maybe you have neurodiversity issues to overcome. Maybe you were bullied or felt out of step socially. There are many ways in which we think ourselves at a disadvantage.

See if you can reframe your challenges as experiences that built up your capa-bilities—and the specific advantages you've gained from them. For example, if you think you aren't as smart as other people, how have you gotten by? What tools do you have in your bag of tricks that have made you as successful as you are? Are you more resourceful? More creative? Able to seek out resources and ask for help from your peers?

Block out some time, maybe ten minutes, and make two columns on a piece of paper. List the ways that you feel you are an underdog. Then take twenty minutes and re-cast those elements as strengths. Notice that your experiences, even if negative at the time, may have created a positive outcome for you. Can you add these outcomes to your list of strengths?

Get honest about your negative thoughts, limiting beliefs, and bad habits, and ask yourself: Will these serve me in college? If not, redefine those limiting beliefs and replace them with positive ones. Create a new plan for the healthy habits you will adopt. Form a new vision of how you will identify yourself, and come up with a plan to reinforce your new identity.

For example, instead of thinking, "I'm a procrastinator," you can think, "I've been able to accomplish a lot last-minute in the past. I know that this won't work well for me in the future, so I'm going to add early prepara-tion to my bag of tricks. I will set things up and keep on top of my work, so I can really throw myself into mastering my subjects. I will make myself unstoppable!"

And then do it. Do not underestimate the power of self-talk. With practice, those thoughts that create doubt in yourself can be replaced by those that truly empower you, especially when you put in place an action plan to follow. And once you put your plan in place, follow it.

There's a saying: "What got you to Egypt won't get you to the Promised Land." Similarly, what got you into college will not necessarily be enough to keep you there. The demands on you to make it through to graduation will be higher than you've experienced before and you'll need all the resources you've got to meet the challenges you'll face. Once you've identified habits, self-definitions, or approaches that will not serve you on your new adventure, decide now to dump them from your bag.

 **ADD TO YOUR ARSENAL**

If you have the time, add new skills to your arsenal before you go. This may be the first time you are on your own and there are some useful life skills you may not have mastered yet. New capabilities add confidence and will help you feel competent in your independence. The more of these you can learn before you leave, the more comfortable you will be when you are navigating on your own.

Put New Tricks in Your Sack

Use the time between high school graduation and your first day on campus to bolster some life skills. For example:

- <u>Learn to make your bed.</u> Admiral William H. McRaven argues that if you start each day by making your bed, you will set yourself up to have a successful day. (If not that, at least it will be a tidier one). Your roommate may thank you for it too. Practice picking up after yourself. Having a clean and organized space will help you focus and be more productive.

- Learn how to do laundry. Find out which products to use, how to balance the load, and how not to mix whites with reds in hot water (unless for some reason you love the weird, uneven shades of pink that result). Learn which of your clothes can and should go in the dryer, and at what heat level, and which ones definitely should air dry instead. Learn how to air dry without growing mold. (Hint: ventilation is key.)

- Learn to cook a few meals. There will be times, even if you are on a college meal plan, that you may want to cook for yourself, especially if you live off campus. If you and your dormmate have a refrigerator, learn how to clean it and set the proper temperature to keep milk from spoiling. Tupperware is critical to lock up open cereal boxes or other staples, unless you like sharing with the ants and other critters you'll attract.

- Wake up and make it to your appointments on time. Make sure you are capable of waking yourself up in the morning. No one's going to be there to pull you out of bed for your early classes. Know your sleeping needs and commit to getting enough hours per night.

- Take responsibility for your health. Consider any medications you may need and make sure you understand how to access them when you're at college.

- Set up your playlists. While you're at it, why not set up a few playlists of your favorite songs? Music and movement can make or improve your mood, so arm yourself with some ready energy. Think about creating separate lists: one to wake you up and set your mood for the day, one to psych you up before your tests, one to calm you down and prepare you for sleep at the end of the day. Include a party playlist that gets you dancing and never fails to raise your spirits, and a soothing playlist that brings you calm. There's a reason baseball players choose their own song when stepping up to the plate, why bands have opening acts to warm up the crowd, why motivational speakers use pounding upbeat songs before coming onstage—music moves us and makes us move. Choose your anthems that call to you and have them ready to rock when you roll.

Money Money Money

Whether you need to work to support your financial aid package, or whether you have an unlimited budget while you're in school, as you transition to adulthood you will need to learn to deal with money. Many schools have a local banking branch, some with special rates or services for students. Take a look at their offerings and compare them to other banks that have branches close by.

You may want to open a local account and get a debit card. This will let you access ATMs and get cash, which should be your first choice in spending, as it allows you to easily keep a running total of your balance as you spend. If you have a job, you often can have your paychecks deposited directly into your account, which may give you better interest rates or discounted fees (not to mention avoiding delays in depositing your check yourself).

You may be offered a credit card to help you start to build credit. This is a trickier proposition, and you will want to research your options carefully. Some cards have better benefits and costs than others, and you'll want to consider which are best for you. Frequent flyer miles? Cash back? No fees? All of these can be useful; which is best depends on your own personal situation.

CAUTION: Use your credit very sparingly, especially if you are not used to using and paying for a credit card. They make it dangerously easy to spend freely, and difficult to remember how much and how often you've spent until you receive the monthly bill at the end. Even the lowest interest rates on these cards can cause you to get into debt trouble (so much for building up your credit rating!) It may take you years, long after graduation, to dig yourself out. Bad credit can lead to big problems down the line—inability to rent an apartment, buy a house, or get loans. Commit to paying off your credit card bill every month and if there is any way to avoid it, don't let your debt accumulate.

In any event, whether you use a debit card or credit card, you MUST look at your monthly statement. Book a time on your calendar once a month to make sure that this occurs. You'll be able to see how much you are spending (and on what), as well as catch when those "free trial offers" you signed up for online turn into monthly payments automatically deducted from your account when the trial period expires. Pro tip: Set up reminders on your phone to alert you when it's time to cancel free trials. By monitoring your account regularly, you will be able to ensure that no one hacked your account and is withdrawing from it or fraudulently charging you. If you run into these troubles, your local branch office can help you address them, especially if you discover them quickly.

And Now a Word About Actual Packing

Your dorm room is smaller than you think. And you likely will need a LOT less stuff than you think. Many colleges offer a pretty comprehensive packing checklist: Use it and consider carefully how much you will take with you. Do you really need ALL thirty-seven stuffed animals? Your entire footwear collection? All those books? You get the picture.

If you have the chance in advance, coordinate with your roommate(s) about who is bringing the mini-refrigerator, bean bag chair, other essentials and nice-to-haves. You won't need doubles of these items, and you will appreciate having the space to turn around in your room. If you find that you do need something that you missed, you probably can have it shipped to you or you can purchase it (maybe secondhand) while you're there.

Conclusion

Remember Maria? When she looked at her past in a new way, focusing on her strengths rather than on her fears and disappointments, she realized that the constant moving forced her to gain skills that she might otherwise not have had. She learned to be a little—okay, a LOT—more outgoing than she might naturally be.

- *She knew that if she didn't want to eat alone at lunch, she would need to proactively put herself out there. If she didn't want to be alone on Friday nights, she might have to be the one to organize a group to go to the football games, skating rink, or movies.*

- *She learned to pull together groups to play ultimate frisbee, to try out local food trucks, to go to a trivia night.*

- *She knew how to introduce herself and join conversations. Being the new kid so many times gave Maria the empathy to understand that EVERYONE in her freshman class would also feel like the new kid. That they would probably be just as scared and nervous as she was (if not more), and they would probably appreciate her reaching out and being friendly.*

- *Maria learned to find her tribes, those people whose interests and goals matched her unique interests. Of course, it was rare to find someone who shared ALL of her interests (after all, how many people love watching sports, listening to music, engaging in debate and speech AND book clubs?) But she found that there were always some people who shared at least some of her individual interests.*

- *Being the new kid so often also gave her confidence that until she found her community, she could be just fine on her own. She had dented many a new house's garage door hitting a tennis ball to herself; she had discovered authors who opened new worlds through their books. Being alone doesn't have to be lonely.*

Despite the loss and aggravation of the frequent moves, she did learn some valuable skills: self-reliance, confidence, and comfort with change (even if she didn't always get to the "embracing change" part, she did at least know she would survive it). The experiences and strengths she brought with her gave her a foundation on which she could build.

All of us have life experiences, both positive and negative, that we can carry into college as strengths. What you choose to bring, and how you decide to use it, can be a superpower you can summon to support you in your journey.

What's in your duffel bag?

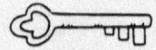 **KEY TIPS**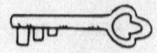

- YOU ALREADY HAVE SKILLS THAT HAVE SUPPORTED YOUR SUCCESS SO FAR. UNDERSTAND AND EMBRACE YOUR CURRENT STRENGTHS, YOUR SUPERPOWERS, AND BE READY TO USE THEM IN YOUR NEW ADVENTURES.

- WE ALL HAVE DOUBTS AND FEARS ABOUT OUR ABILITIES AND WEAKNESSES. THE NEGATIVE THOUGHTS AND SELF-DOUBT YOU HAVE MAY BE BASED ON BAD DATA, OR BE OUT OF DATE. REFRAME YOUR NEGATIVES AND DUMP THE DEADWEIGHT.

- YOU HAVE TIME TO GAIN NEW SKILLS THAT WILL HELP YOU ON YOUR JOURNEY. PREPARE YOURSELF FOR "ADULTING" AND STUFF YOUR SACK WITH NEW SKILLS BEFORE YOU GO. EACH NEW COMPETENCY WILL GIVE YOU ONE LESS THING TO WORRY ABOUT, AND ONE MORE THING TO BUILD YOUR CONFIDENCE.

Chapter 3

PLOT YOUR COURSE(S)

"A goal without a plan is just a wish."
—Antoine de Saint-Exupéry

Susannah sat in the hall outside her college guidance counselor's office, anxious and upset. This was going to be her fourth time switching majors, and this time it looked like she definitely might have to push out her graduation another year.

She thought about the call she had had with her parents last night. Her mother's silent disapproval weighed on her almost as heavily as her dad's yelling. "Susannah, when are you going to grow up?" he'd huffed. "I am paying for a very expensive education so that you will make something of yourself," he'd puffed. She could picture his red face and bulging eyes clearly in her mind. "You can't just hide out in college forever," he'd blown up, at *a decibel level usually reserved for rock concerts. "This is the last time, so you'd better be sure." He'd then slammed down the phone.*

Susannah was so disheartened. The truth was that she still wasn't sure. She had tried to find her passion, she really had. She'd taken those aptitude tests in high school, but they hadn't helped her find her true purpose. She was good at and interested in a lot of things, but nothing had grabbed her soul. She'd taken a wide variety of general ed classes, and "Intro to…" classes, and a smattering of other lower division classes, and although many things were interesting, no one subject stuck out as the one and only thing for her. And now here she was, almost at the end of her first semester junior year, and she felt just as lost as she had felt when she had come in as a freshman.

Susannah's predicament is not unusual, but no one wants to be in her place in their junior year.

So how can you avoid this mess, especially if you don't already know your passion going in to college? Or maybe even worse, what if you THOUGHT you had your passion going in and have now discovered that maybe it isn't your passion after all?

So far, we've talked about defining your preliminary goals and understanding your underlying motivational "whys." Now, before you put your hands on the steering wheel and start off down the road, make sure you plan the route you will choose to get you there. In this Chapter, you'll find the tools to create your overall map to your destination and make your preliminary plan.

BEGIN BEFORE YOU BEGIN

Your first step is to research your options, and take a broad view of the mountain you want to climb. Think of this as the high level, bird's-eye view that sets the boundaries and will contain your more detailed potential step-by-step paths to the summit. This view will show the overall context of what it takes to graduate and the routes that can take you there. It will provide the foundation for your plan.

Survey the Landscape

Take notes as you research. Look through the list of majors, minors, and certificate programs, and their respective requirements. Some colleges won't let you declare a major until certain pre-requisites are met; some colleges require you to have declared a major prior to your acceptance. In either event, you'll want to understand the specific classes required, the number of upper class units required, the general education requirements, and the elective courses available to you.

If you are attending community or junior college and plan to transfer into a four-year university, you will also want to know which courses are transferable, and what the application requirements and deadlines are for the colleges to which you want to apply. It will help you avoid having to duplicate courses, and help you track transfer requirements, such as recommendations from your professors, if needed.

Next, look through the current course catalog. Note those courses that look particularly interesting to you, the semesters that they are offered, and where they would fit toward graduation requirements. For example, does the course fulfill a requirement toward your major or a general education requirement? Is it a required course or an elective?

Pay attention to whether it is offered every semester or year. Is it offered by a number of professors or only one? By a faculty member or by a visiting professor? Is the class held in a large lecture hall or offered as a small group seminar? All of this background research will help you form a broad outline of possibilities.

 ## What to do if You Don't Know What You Want

Sometimes you simply need more time, and maybe more life, before you know what you want to do "for life." Sometimes you'll change your mind about what you want to do later in life, after college, regardless of your major. It is becoming increasingly common for people to change careers in their lifetime. Changes in technology, advances in knowledge across disciplines, the global workplace, society in general....There are constant changes that may impact your future and future work. If you hold onto anything in this section, it should be this: Picking a major is not a life sentence! You can change your mind before, or even after, you graduate.

Don't stress about not knowing your passion, or having a "forever" major. Pick something that allows you to play to your strengths and gives you flexibility for future choices, and then master it. Philosophy majors can get into med school; physics majors can make strong marketers. You are gaining life skills, not serving a life sentence.

Rather than look at your major as the final end, see it as a step along your life journey. If you don't know which path to take, look at the path that offers you something you currently value or one that will give you the opportunity to gain knowledge or capabilities that will serve you in life. Play to your strengths and strengthen your play. Hone your skills to a deeper level of mastery and rest confident that your skills will serve you in the future, even if it may not be as you originally imagined.

Ch-Ch-Changes: Dealing with Uncertainty is a Critical Skill

"Change is inevitable. Growth is optional."
—John Maxwell

Learning how to move forward through uncertainty is a supremely valuable skill. Think about the amount of disruption you've already experienced in your life, and know that **nothing is constant but change**. The COVID-19 pandemic brought about cataclysmic changes to school and daily life for a whole generation and there have been financial, political, entertainment, social media, and technology shifts that may have impacted you as well. With each of these shifts, large and small, you've had to adapt and learn new things. Time and opportunities don't stand still. If you can teach yourself to be able to adjust on the fly, while keeping to your true north, you will have gained a very valuable skill that will serve you throughout your life.

At some point, you will need to make a decision on a major and stick to it through to the end (or at least through graduation). One critical guideline when you make this decision: Make up your mind in a moment of strength; don't change it in a moment of weakness. Think through your decisions when you are calm and clear-headed. Don't drop the whole course or change your major just because you flubbed one paper. Consider your options, alternatives, and the potential impact of your decision. Then, once you've made up your mind, go for it. Go all in, and give it all you've got. Don't give in to second-guessing or doubts; stay the course through to the end, comfortable that it doesn't have to be the end for you forever.

Learning to hold course to the finish line also is important, though. One of the reasons that employers value college graduates is that, if nothing else, you've proven that you can go the distance. You survived obstacles and increasingly difficult courses, and you didn't quit. You will have taken action, met deadlines, completed projects and papers. You will have have pushed yourself past uncertainty, boredom, time pressure, and mental pressure. The mere fact that you made it through will say something great about you. If you count the skills you add along the way, you will be much better off for having taken a path to its conclusion, even if you take a different direction later in life.

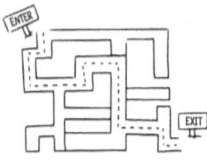 ## MAP YOUR MILESTONES

Take the research you did when you surveyed the landscape above. Using your prospective (or placeholder) major's requirements, construct a preliminary general map of the major milestones you need to reach. Include the prerequisites for the courses, the progression of classes leading up to graduation. Be sure to include the number of credits required and whether they are lower or upper-level classes. Check the requirements and timing for declaring a major. Use this map to design a more detailed, step-by-step plan that can take you through graduation.

If you don't know your major, pick one as a placeholder just to let you form a path so you can have a workable plan at the outset. It may not be the ultimate plan, but you've got a starting point and direction to guide your journey.

Plan Your Itinerary

Once you pick your path, you will create more detailed plans. Look at the courses you'll take for the upcoming semester (or quarter), and while you're at it, take a look out at the semesters (or quarters) that will come later. Plan your way all the way through the four years. Note which courses are offered only once a year and when they are offered.

Consider which courses have prerequisites that must be taken in a certain order. Come up with a preliminary itinerary that details the steps of a path that can take you through graduation.

If you are attending a community college, you may need to break up your planning into two stages: first, to plan what you want to accomplish while at your community college (including understanding the transfer requirements, transfer application requirements and deadlines); and second to make sure that the work you are doing now will advance you towards your degree. You may not be able to plan your upper division courses (they may vary by school), but you can research what it takes to major in your proposed field across prospective universities, and build your plan from that.

Remember that this is a preliminary plan! Some courses offered today may not be offered tomorrow. Professors move on to other colleges, or retire, or are retired. Subject matter and requirements change over time as well: For example, the courses required to graduate with a computer science major may change as new technologies and programming languages emerge and disrupt old ones. New majors may be created along the way as well, as new specialties surface and new opportunities arise. You may decide to change your plan as your knowledge and experience expands along the way.

The true value in having a preliminary plan is to have a path that sets your direction, against which you can evaluate opportunities and changes as they arise. A critical note: Every time you make changes to your plan, go through the process again of checking requirements and prerequisites, so that your changes don't have the unintended consequence of jeopardizing your timely graduation.

Dabble with Dedication

Your time in college is the perfect opportunity to explore new subjects and classes. That's part of what is so great about having a college experience. But it is important not to confuse dabbling in diverse subjects with wasting time. Approach testing the waters and trying new things with dedication, not just skimming the surface.

Steve Jobs famously took a calligraphy class at his college. He was not enrolled at the time, but was auditing various courses that caught his interest. He applied himself with diligence and mastered the nuances of how beautiful letters integrate with design. When he took the class, he had no idea that it would become integral to Apple's approach to product design. So although the class did not appear immediately relevant, the skills Jobs learned in his class had a huge impact on his future and success.

This can be true for you, too. Take courses that interest you, even if they are outside of your major or expertise. Study hard and learn what you can from them. Make use of your general education class requirements and electives, and make this learning count. You never know how much you can benefit from this knowledge later in life.

Every college has classes that have the reputation of being easy, whether they are called "gut" classes or "freebies" or whatever the term is at your particular school. These are the filler classes that people take to meet their general education requirements, to bolster their GPA, or to make their schedule easier while meeting the minimum course load. A word about these "gut"' classes: Unless they are in a subject that is interesting to you, don't waste your time. What's easy for some isn't always easy for others and may not be easy for you. And why waste your tuition just to get an "easy" A? There are many paths up the mountain, and you have your own path to your goals. Maximize your chance to learn as much as you can about anything and everything that will be useful to you. Remember why you are here and stick to your own plan.

Consider Foreign Travel Early

Many colleges offer study abroad opportunities, either through the college itself or in affiliation with other universities. And colleges that don't have their own study abroad programs often will accept transfer credit for certain courses taught abroad. Living and learning in a foreign country can be an amazing experience and college can be the perfect time to do this.

Would you like to take a quarter, semester, summer, or even year to immerse yourself abroad? If you're at all tempted, run, don't walk, to research what your college has to offer as soon as possible. There are a number of things to consider and arrangements to make before you can go. Some places have extensive language requirements and some have none at all (you take classes to learn the language while you are there). Some places have certain courses that they teach during certain semesters or quarters. Some offer only general education courses, while some are geared toward upper-level students. Some may have prerequisites beyond language that you'll need to meet.

You'll want to think about the courses and timing on offer and see how they best fit into YOUR plan. Students typically will take their study abroad during sophomore or junior year. In some colleges, you don't declare your major until junior year, but some majors have a specific progression or cadence of classes and prerequisites that would make it difficult to go abroad without delaying your graduation. In that case, if you know that you'd like to go abroad, you might want to go during your sophomore year or over the summer. Depending on the program, you may need to apply during your freshman year! Many students miss out on the opportunity because they don't think to apply early enough. If you explore this option early, you can make plans to optimize the best timing for you.

CHALLENGE #7: MAP YOUR MILESTONES

Your goal in this challenge is to understand your college's graduation requirements and the options available to you. First, look through the list of majors, minors, and certificate programs, and their respective requirements. Take notes as you go. Some colleges won't let you declare a major until certain prerequisites are met; some colleges require you to have declared a major prior to your acceptance. In either event, you'll want to understand the specific classes required, the number of upper class units required, the general education requirements, and the elective courses available to you.

Next you will want to look through the course catalog and note any particular classes (or professors) that interest you. Check the student reviews of the classes. Look over the class syllabus and reading material, if available.

Even if you are not completely convinced that your major is going to be your one true passion, you need to pick a target that is close enough: to your interests, to your strengths, with the widest applicability to jobs or future skills. So if you don't know your ultimate destination, define those skills and experiences that will benefit you in a broader sense.

For example, many paths can benefit from solid skills in public speaking, so maybe you'll want to take a course on that. Or maybe you'd like to learn how to build presentations, gain marketing skills, or study business finance. Many of these types of courses can fill your general education requirements and will build useful capabilities along the way. Pick the one preferred path that resonates best for you for now, resting confident that there are alternative routes if you need them.

Remember, your college may change the majors offered, the requirements for those majors, and the courses offered throughout your journey.

So look at this exercise as a way to form the big picture and starting point for making your plans. As you progress along your path, check back to make sure that all of the pieces of your plan still work. Make adjustments as new, more intriguing courses are offered; or as current classes are no longer available—always with the view of what it takes to graduate.

Set Your Mental Map

Have you seen movies or video games where the hero stops time in his or her mind, then plots out the next steps to victory, to escape, or to take other actions? Then time speeds up and the character acts as he or she envisioned? Success often begins with visualizing the steps you can take to reach your goals. You, too, can employ this technique to make a mental map to your success.

A mental map is one that you create in your mind to help you firmly establish your path to your goals. Starting from where you are now, you look forward. You imagine your ultimate destination and the steps you'll need to get you there. You see yourself taking the steps and succeeding along the way. You remember your strengths and tap into the confidence they bring as you plan ahead.

Your mental map may have some planned stops along the way. If you can't see all the way to your final goal yet, you can envision planned stops to assess where you are, and confirm you are on the right path. Your planned stops can also act as milestones to mark your progress. A strong mental map can increase your chances of success, if you:

- Build a clear vision of a future that is compelling to you and picture the steps you can take to get there.

- Imagine what you'll need to accomplish those steps and mentally prepare yourself.

- Take consistent action and steps towards your goals.

You can add power your mental map by creating a personal morning mantra: a positive statement that you repeat to yourself that inspires you to reach your goals. You CAN do this! Repeat this to yourself with conviction every morning when you rise, and start your day in the right frame of mind to progress along your journey.

Forecast Your Future Success

Have you ever heard that your mind doesn't know the difference between what you've actually experienced and what you imagine visually? The more vivid and detailed your vision is, the less your body distinguishes between your vision and reality. Your body experiences your vision much the same as a memory, as if it has already happened. Visualizing the future, or "future casting," is a powerful technique used by many successful and high-achieving people as they plan their future.

Future casting is different from your mental map. In your mental map, you are envisioning your route and the steps you need to take looking forward. In future casting, you see yourself at the journey's end, basking in the success, as if it has already occurred, and then look back at your journey. Future casting presumes your accomplishments have been achieved.

Let's be clear: Merely imagining that you've absorbed the course material and done the course work versus actually doing it are two different things. You've got to do the work! But when you future cast, your brain will be on board and looking for ways to make your imagined future a reality. It gives an extra boost to your commitment, and confidence to see your journey through. When you future cast and then add the detailed steps in your mental map, you will have created a path that can lead to your success. Take committed action on your path, and you will get to your destination.

CHALLENGE #8: FUN WITH FUTURECASTING

Try this: Imagine yourself one year from now, having successfully completed your freshman year. Draw and color in that picture in your mind with as much detail as possible: Perhaps you are laughing with a group of friends, or you've just received your final grades and made the Dean's List again for the second semester. You've boxed up your belongings to store over the summer. You feel happy and healthy and confident and strong. Imagine the sun on your face, the blue sky, the wind gently blowing. You think back on the goals you set, the steps you took to achieve them, the decisions and connections you made, your hard work. You think back on the challenges you faced, how you never gave up, the lessons you learned, and how you've grown. Imagine how great it feels and bask in the glow it gives you.

Now create your mental map. Go back to the list of goals you created in the first challenge. For each goal, list the steps that it will take to accomplish them. Note the progression of courses, the resources, the timing of each step. For example, if going overseas is one of your goals, plot out how you can integrate that into the rest of your plans. If graduating with honors is your goal, what actions will you take to make sure that you are on track with your courses? How will you correct your plan if you are not making top grades along the way? If you are in sports or band or theater or student government, how can you make room for that commitment and still meet your other goals?

Start with the viewpoint at the successful end, your future cast, and then map out a path to that success that you can follow. Notice what you think will be easy and also what will require you to stretch yourself. Then take action! Follow the steps you imagined having taken. Use this map as your guide, but don't be afraid to course correct if your path, or your steps, aren't getting you to your destination.

Maybe you underestimated the time commitments for the clubs or studying, or the amount of time needed to write a strong paper or prepare for tests. Maybe transitioning between subjects takes longer than you expected or you encounter unexpected obstacles. In this case, start again with the end in mind and revise your mental map, so that you always have a plan to get you to your destination.

Training Your Brain Bias

It has been said that nothing is more expensive than a missed opportunity. Having a mental map sets your success mindset and conditions you to see opportunities that you might otherwise miss. Your mind can only focus on a limited number of things amid the vast number of inputs, so by identifying those items that are most important to you, your mind will gravitate toward them. In effect, you set your mind to filter out irrelevant information and hone in on data that matters.

To test how this works, think about something new that you bought or were given recently: a new pair of Nike shoes, for example. Focus on it: the color, size, model, or other attributes. Now pay attention to how often you notice other people with the same shoes. It suddenly seems like everyone has the same Nikes, because your brain is now biased to notice them.

This same phenomenon can work to your advantage in college, as you train your brain to look for ways to achieve your goals. You'll become aware of guest speakers on campus, or people who share your same passions, or part-time jobs in your future field, or networking opportunities. You will tune in to subjects and course work that furthers you on your path. Your mental map sets up subconscious focus and puts you ahead of the game.

 ## OUTSMART OVERWHELM AT THE OUTSET

"All work and no play" creates stress and won't work in the long run. "All play and weak work" creates stress too and isn't sustainable either. So the key is to be balanced and realistic. Think about planning your workload with this in mind.

Unless you are an avid reader or are jammed against graduation requirements, don't take all courses with heavy reading all together in one semester. Or all classes that require lab work. Try to break up the monotony with a mix. Throw in a "just for fun" class if your schedule permits, such as yoga, beginning dance, or an exercise class. If you can't fit in a full course, make time to join an intramural sport or form an ultimate frisbee or other pick-up game—anything that you would find fun and that would allow you to get physical and give your brain a break.

If you aren't an art or music major, think about adding a short course in music or art, to give you time and space to enhance your creativity and take a break from your core studies. (And if you ARE a music or art major, think about taking a computer science or math class to switch things up.) The point is to build in a break from the routine, an opportunity to take a different perspective, and a chance to develop new skills.

Variety is the spice of life, so make sure you have some spice in your college life. Take courses that interest YOU. Challenge yourself to look outside your comfort zone and try new things. (If you're really worried, you may be able to take the course pass/fail).

A Well-Planned Journey Leads to Good Places

When you are planning your slate of courses, don't forget to think about logistics. Consider your course load balance: Don't stack all heavy courses upon each other, especially when you're just starting out. Sometimes you can't avoid taking tough classes together, say if you are on a particular pre-med or engineering track. If this is the case, try to add a course or two in a very different vein to break things up. A creative writing course or beginning drawing or some type of P.E. course— yoga, badminton, anything—can provide general education units and a shift from the bulk of your studies.

Consider the distance between classrooms. Will you need to scramble to make it on time? Will you have a chance to read over your class notes before the next class starts? Will you have time to get a snack or a drink of water? Know yourself and how well you transition. If it takes you longer to collect yourself and get your things together, what can you do to make it easier?

What time of day are the courses offered? And how does that mesh with your natural learning strengths? Shakespeare said, "To thine own self be true." Although he wasn't talking about early morning classes, his advice works here. Know your natural peak study time. Are you a morning person? Do you find that you concentrate best shortly after you wake up, but your attention flags in the afternoon? If you are a morning person and think best in the early part of the day, try to take morning classes.

Or are you a night person, who really doesn't come alive until late afternoon, but find your best concentration is around 10 p.m.? If you know that you can't get up in the morning, don't book an 8 a.m. class! You'll sleep through it, either physically or mentally, which definitely won't help you learn the material. If you cannot get up early, even after setting several alarms, maybe morning classes aren't the best for you.

If you are wiped out by the end of the week, Friday afternoon classes may not be wise. You may want to load up on classes at the beginning of the week. Or if you operate best with a steady stream of information, spread out your classes with breaks in between to absorb the material as you go.

Don't forget: One key element for success in college is to actually ATTEND your classes. So to the extent you can, schedule your classes around your natural preferences.

Make sure to plan when you will have time to eat. Thinking hard is hard work, and you will need sustenance to survive it. You also will need time for physical activity to give your brain a break and amp up your metabolism. The best learning comes when you are focused. You need nourishing food and movement to perform at your best.

So how do you know when your plan is well-made? When it:

1. is in line with your "why"

2. moves you forward toward your goals

3. is balanced in terms of course demands

4. allows sufficient time for you to perform well on your assignments

5. includes time for eating, exercising, socializing, and relaxing

CHALLENGE # 9: PLOT YOUR PATH

Once you have your schedule of classes for the semester or quarter, make a map of your planned week:

1. Create a grid in landscape view on a piece of paper or online calendar. On the left-hand side and on the vertical, create blocks beginning with 7 a.m. through 10 p.m. Across the top on the horizontal, create space for each day of the week, beginning with Monday. This creates a view of your "week at a glance."

2. Next, color coordinate class blocks (for example yellow is Freshman English, MWF from 9-10; red is Intro to Biology MWF 1:30- 3:00 with Bio Lab Th 2-4; etc). Place these time blocks on your foundational grid. This will give you an easy visual, and will make clear the open blocks of time you have to work with.

3. Next, layer in the other essentials. Consider travel time to and from classes. Knowing that there are 168 hours in a week, build in time to eat, work out, study, and socialize—you can color code these too, if it helps you picture your schedule.

4. If there are special events that you know are coming up—Parents' Weekend, Homecoming, Battle of the Bands—block those into your calendar as well. That will help you later, as you know in advance that you will have less study time over that weekend or event. This becomes critical as you receive your big assignments and test dates. If you know in advance that there is a conflict, you can plan your study time accordingly and avoid a lot of stress.

Be honest with yourself! If you know that you plan to party hard after the football games, block off time Saturday morning to sleep in and recover. If you know that it takes you longer than some to read, and you have a lot of classes with heavy reading, schedule extra time for studying and block in some mental breaks to rest your eyes and keep your focus fresh. This plan is your plan, so you'll only cheat yourself if you don't plan this out thoughtfully and create a schedule that works with your unique strengths and needs.

So now you may be thinking, "I'm not the kind of person who's going to make a color-coded grid for anything. This is not going to work for me." If you aren't a grid-maker, that's okay. But you still can use whatever planning and organization techniques DO work for you to set yourself up to achieve your goals. Once you get the hang of planning this way, it becomes easier and easier to do.

One other point: Color-coordinated or not, this is not a "set it and forget it" exercise. As with any plan, to get the most out of it, consult it regularly and revise it if and as circumstances change. Several things can happen as you progress down your path. For example:

- You may have underestimated the amount of time if takes to travel between classes.

- You may discover a dedicated study group that you'd like to add to your schedule.

- You may like to build in TA office hours for a class or add a new club to your regular weekly routine.

- You may need to build in more down time.

If you keep your plan up to date, you will have a nice baseline that you can use to evaluate new opportunities as they arise. It will let you see if you will be overcommitted. You will be able to easily assess: Can you manage the additional responsibilities or workload, or attend that party or event and still perform your best?

Pre-Registration Power Work

Many college students find registering for classes overwhelming. There are hundreds of courses offered each semester or quarter. How are you supposed to pick the ones that are right for you?

One useful trick is to work toward the middle of your schedule from both ends. Start with what is required and non-negotiable. Does your school require every incoming freshman to take "College Writing 101" if they don't test out of it? Put that on your list. All your other options are going to have to fit around that. Next look to general ed requirements. Are there specific courses that you have to take to graduate that it helps to take at the beginning of your college journey? Are there prerequisites for classes you want to take as soon as possible? Put one or two of these options on your list. Look at the times they're offered. Now you've got something to talk to your advisor or guidance counselor about. This will get you started.

Register as early as you can for each term's classes. Many courses have prerequisites, and if those fill up without you in them, you may be taking the one at 8 a.m.—if you get in at all! If they close without you in them, you might miss out on your preferred course choices, or even have to delay graduation. Luck favors the prepared, so put yourself in place to be lucky and stay on top of the enrollment schedule. And have a plan B if your preferred courses fill before you get in.

Know What You Need: Self-Care to Take You There

You've got your preliminary destination and goals planned, you know the strengths and skills you're bringing on your journey. Now it's time to consider what support you may need along the way. Think in four dimensions: physical, mental, social, and academic.

Whether this means planning for regular fitness breaks, ensuring you have proper sleep habits, or scheduling in downtime just for you, be sure to understand and address your physical needs.

- Eat well. You don't have to be a nut about nutrition, but it is true that nourishing your body nourishes your brain. Try to eat regularly—and not always junk! Drink water. Lots and lots of water.

- Sleep well. Get enough sleep regularly. Yes, you will have late nights, some of which will be followed by early mornings. But don't fall for the myth that you'll make it up over the weekend, or next week, or next month. It's just not true. One of best things that you can do to reduce your stress and emotional spikes, put in your best efforts, and achieve to your highest potential, is to get proper amounts of sleep. What's the proper amount? That depends on you. Some people function on six hours, some need ten. The people who tell you they can operate at peak capacity on four hours are fooling themselves and you. If you can manage consistently to get the amount of sleep you personally need, you will be amazed at how much better you will function and feel.

- Get exercise. Almost all colleges have some kind of fitness center and many offer various classes at no-or-low-cost to students. If you don't want to trek to the fitness center, think about video games as a fun way to exercise. No, not the games that keep you glued to your bed or couch for hours, but ones that get you up and moving. Zumba Fitness, World Party (Xbox), Arms

(Nintendo Switch), Beat Saber (PlayStation), classic Punch-Out (Wii), and many more offer a nice break that will get your heart pumping.

Another perk of fitness gaming is that you can compete virtually or exercise alongside a friend somewhere else, as long as both parties have the game and an internet connection. Games like Just Dance, Arms, and Beat Saber all have multiplayer capabilities. Enrolling a friend to join you may ramp up the fun and keep you accountable. When it comes to exercise, strive for consistency and switch it up if the routine becomes boring. Explore workout apps and YouTube videos, IG posts, and other sources on your phone or tablet to find the ones that inspire you most, and build time to get physical into your schedule.

Going for walks or hiking with friends is a great way to combine exercise and socializing. Get out into nature if you can; get your heart pumping and breathe some fresh air. Find something that you enjoy and make it a part of your routine.

- Practice good hygiene. Wash your hands regularly, brush and floss your teeth, take showers with soap, and launder your clothes. Your roommates, classmates, and even those passing by on the footpaths will thank you for it.

- Socialize! Find people you have things in common with and join clubs and affinity groups. You won't survive the marathon if you don't take time to enjoy the journey with others along the way.

- Guard your personal well-being. Explore your school's resources for mental health, physical health, and academic support in advance to know what's available for you. Bake into your schedule the time and events (and non-event "chill" time) to let yourself relax and give your mind a break.

Sometimes, despite your best planning, the stress threatens to take over. Your mind races, you can't relax, and it feels like you're about to have a panic attack. Too many deadlines, too much pressure, too little time, too little sleep…What do you do when it's all too much?!

First step: Breathe. Put down what you are carrying (mentally and physically) and free yourself to breathe. Take ten deep breaths, slowly in and slowly out. Of course, breathing alone won't solve all of your problems. But it will give you a moment to pause and take stock of where you are.

If you just can't relax and are so overwhelmed that you are finding it difficult to function, reach out to your university's health and wellness center and get help! This is NOT the time to go it alone, and you are not the only one who experiences this from time to time. Know that there are resources to help you through this rough patch and that there is a smoother path ahead. Reach out and use the resources available to you to get you through more quickly.

Understand this: The more anxious you are, the worse your decision-making capability is. So, know in advance that if you find yourself in a panic or feeling depressed, your thinking capacity has been hijacked for a moment. Don't make any major decisions while you're in that state, other than to get help! Share your thoughts and seek support. The perspective of others may help you see new ways to evaluate your situation and your options and help you process your feelings.

Master Self-Advocacy

Some students face certain challenges that can't easily be resolved by themselves. For example, students with learning disabilities, physical disabilities, health issues, and so on, may require personalized help. There can be very real challenges, some of which need special attention regularly and some of which only on occasion. These challenges are often not insurmountable and can be managed with care and planning. If you have particular needs:

- ***Plan*** in advance ***whenever possible***.

- ***Communicate*** with the people involved with the solution ***as soon as possible***.

- ***Coordinate*** with the proper resources at your school ***as often as possible***.

Take ownership and empower yourself to explore the resources available to you. Actively and proactively seek out the assistance you need to succeed. Whether or not you have chronic conditions or simply need additional support from time to time, colleges have support systems (tutoring centers, resources and clubs for students with learning disabilities, etc.) to help students with diverse learning needs. But they will not necessarily come to you. **It is up to you to know your needs and to advocate for yourself.** Self-advocacy is a skill that can serve everyone, and one that, once mastered, can benefit you for your entire life.

Conclusion

Remember Susannah? As she waited for her appointment with her advisor, she looked down the hall at the large number of students all waiting for their appointments.

She thought about how long it took her to get around to scheduling her appointment. Now that it was the end of the semester, it seemed like all of the counselors had full calendars. This week was the final deadline to declare a major.

Why hadn't she reached out before? Her previous meetings with her assigned guidance counselor had been pleasant. She hadn't even bothered to meet with her department advisor. Why had she been so resistant to taking advantage of the resources available to her? Looking at it now, she wished she had been more involved and proactive.

When it was her turn, Susannah's counselor, Jessie, greeted her with a smile. Susannah took a deep breath and unloaded all her fears, doubts, and confusion. When she finally wound down, Jessie said, "Wow, that's a lot to unpack. Let's look at what you have done up to now and see what we're working with." During the next fifty minutes, they identified areas of Susannah's particular interest and her preferred ways of learning. Together, they evaluated the requirements for different majors and considered the courses Susannah had taken already. They talked about combining majors into an independent study path, and what that would take.

As they talked, Susannah found herself drawn to one major and became excited about the path they mapped out to take her through to graduation. She would be able to graduate on time and she could see clearly how to get there. She'd be taking courses that inspired her to learn! She understood where there was flexibility, and still room to make changes. At the end of the hour, Susannah promised to keep in touch with Jessie, and felt that she had found not only a solution, but also a trusted ally.

Have you ever heard the saying, "You can lead a horse to water, but you can't make him drink"? There is a wealth of resources available to you as a student, but only you, yourself, can make you seek them out and use them. People with experience, knowledge, and wisdom are waiting to be your sounding board. You don't need to take their advice if it doesn't resonate with you, but why not brainstorm with the best?

There are career counselors and tutors, professors, department administrators…so many people to help you on your journey. And if you pick a time to talk with them during the semester that isn't jammed against a deadline, you'll find that they will be happy to help you figure it out—whether "it" is choosing your major, learning how to study effectively, deciding what to focus on in your class, or whatever else "it" may be for you. If you take charge of your success, you will find many people willing to help you on your path.

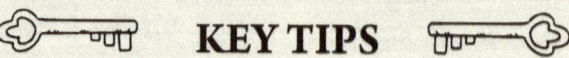

KEY TIPS

- RESEARCH THE MAJORS, REQUIRED COURSES, ELECTIVES, AND UNITS TO GET TO KNOW YOUR OPTIONS. IF YOU ARE GOING TO A COMMUNITY COLLEGE AND PLAN TO TRANSFER TO A 4-YEAR UNIVERSITY, KNOW THE TRANSFER REQUIRE- MENTS AND DEADLINES.

- MAP OUT YOUR MILESTONES FOR A FOUR-YEAR PLAN, INCLUDING COURSE PREREQUISITES AND PROGRESSION.

- OUTSMART THE LIKELIHOOD THAT YOU'LL BECOME OVERWHELMED. THINK ABOUT LOGISTICS AND YOUR WORKLOAD. INCLUDE YOUR ACADEMIC, AND ALSO PHYSICAL, SOCIAL, SPIRITUAL, AND EMOTIONAL GOALS TO HELP KEEP YOUR BALANCE. PLOT YOUR ITINERARY AND FOLLOW IT TO YOUR DESTINATION.

Chapter 4

EXPLORING THE KNOWN, THE UNKNOWN, AND THE PLACES IN BETWEEN

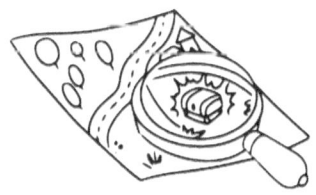

"You miss 100% of the shots you don't take."
—Wayne Gretzky

The first in his family to attend university, Jean-Carlos was committed to making the most of his adventure. He had also never been out of the country, so he was super excited for his first trip to Japan as part of his school's overseas studies program. He had attended all of the meetings, gotten his passport, and chosen his classes. He had even arranged for a part-time work-study job teaching English to Japanese students while he was there, to help defray some of the costs. As soon as his plane landed, he couldn't wait to explore! Everyone else was tired from the plane ride and wanted to rest up before classes started the next day, so he headed off on his own, planning to see a museum a few metro stops from the international dorm.

Jean-Carlos headed to the metro station on the corner. As he peered up at the sign, he realized that figuring out the directions was going to be a LOT harder than he thought. The Japanese characters were complex and looked so similar to one another! It was impossible to figure out. Surrounded by hordes of people rushing around, Jean-Carlos decided that his best bet would be to count subway stops to his destination. He'd take his chances, hoping he'd get off at the correct stop.

He was immediately caught up in the swarm of the crowd as the train pulled into the station. Jean-Carlos was propelled forward and before he knew it, he was on the train. The doors had closed with a whoosh and the train blasted out of the station.

Disoriented, he went several stops before he realized that he had completely forgotten to count. So what to do? It took a few more stops for Jean-Carlos to gather his courage and exit the train. He found himself somewhere in the middle of Tokyo, on a crowded street, with no museum in sight. With no GPS, he decided to make the best of it and wander.

He noticed a local Kabuki theater with a matinee show and purchased a ticket for the balcony. The makeup and costumes were elaborate, and the acting was over the top. Perfect, since Jean-Carlos did not understand a word! The audience yelled and cheered and booed and laughed throughout the loud and exuberant performance. They seemed to have a fabulous time and Jean-Carlos did too, watching the audience as much as the actors on stage and thinking about the serendipity that brought him there….

Whether you're traveling to college in your hometown, or a new city, state, or country, you will become more comfortable as you become more familiar with your surroundings. There's a lot to discover—about yourself, your studies, your campus and beyond. Sometimes the rewards will be biggest when you stretch your boundaries and explore the unexpected.

DON'T DISS ORIENTATION

Take advantage of freshman orientation. This is one of the fastest ways to get a feel for campus and all it has to offer. Stay open to possibilities and get yourself out there to explore your new world.

Some campuses offer formal pre-orientation programs that typically take place during the late summer before school starts. These can be mini-courses, or camping or hiking tours, themed get-togethers, meet and greets, or other activities. If time and finances allow, consider whether joining one of these programs or events could be beneficial to you. And if so—GO!

In the first week, there will be many events: some put on by the school itself, some by departments within the school, some by dorms and dorm clusters, some by various clubs. Force yourself to go to as many of these as you can. This is one time where most people are new, like you, and everyone is roughly in the same boat. These events are set up to showcase campus resources, opportunities, and affinity groups. They make it easy to meet people and become acclimated to the campus.

Be curious, be brave, and explore. You may find that you are completely uninterested in some of the offerings, maybe many of them. But some may appeal to you, and you may discover a new interest that you hadn't considered before. Whether you dip in a toe or dive in fully, the pool is open and the water is fine.

Tour Like a Tourist

Tour your campus before classes start and familiarize yourself with the campus layout: where your classes are, where the food is, and where the library is. Suss out the rules for the fitness center, library carrel sign-ups, and resource centers (health, study resources, financial aid). Set up your bank accounts. Familiarize yourself with local bus routes and put the bus schedule app on your phone. Gather what you need and make yourself comfortable in your environment.

When in Doubt, Go to the Campus Bookstore and Student Union

Not everyone knows this, but the college bookstore is a great resource. If something is happening on campus, chances are you will find a flyer for it, guide to it, or tickets for it at your college bookstore.

Peruse the bulletin board and roam the aisles. Are there food and drinks for late night snacks? Super school swag you absolutely need? Study guides or summary sheets for some of your tough classes? You may find that the bookstore is the answer to your "I'm new at school and can't find it" questions. The same goes for the Student Union. Check them out and see what's on offer.

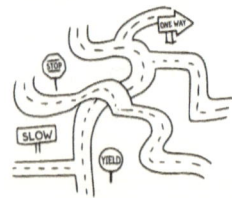 ## BOULEVARDS, EXPRESSWAYS, AND THE BEATEN PATHS

One major advantage in college is that likely others have gone before you and established a trail that you can follow. For example, many majors have a set of courses and a particular order that paves the way to get you from here to there. Some courses will have labs, or organized study groups, or supplemental reading or other resources to guide you along your way. Many colleges have their own student and communication networks: websites or other portals where you can find the school calendar, special events, job fairs, and other announcements.

Many professors have their own networks as well, where they post key class information such as the syllabus and assignments.

Your college has systems designed to facilitate your journey. Take the time to understand what's available, in to those resources useful for you. Sign on to the student portal to know the deadlines, the process for adding or dropping classes and when tuition payments are due. Be proactive! **The roads have been built, but it is up to you to know how and when to drive on them.**

Working the Job

Working on campus is another avenue to explore. Some financial aid packages include a work study component that guarantees a job—but they don't require any particular one. Because not all campus jobs are equal, consider the differences in jobs in light of what matters most to you.

Some jobs may pay more, while others may have benefits like gratuities or employee discounts. For example, being a waiter in the faculty club may offer tips or gratuities in addition to the base pay. The dorm dining hall may offer free meals to its workers.

There are non-monetary benefits to explore, too. Some jobs let you study while working, for example at the library desk if there are no students checking in. Some may offer you experience in the area you are studying. Some jobs have fixed hours, which can help when you're creating your schedule; some offer variable hours that can flex week to week to help you manage your workload during finals.

Apart from the financial benefits, a part-time job on or off campus can give you the opportunity to demonstrate work skills, obtain a reference, and meet other college students.

Think about the elements that matter most to you as you research the job openings and decide to where you'd like to apply.

Food Glorious Food

Not all dining halls are equal—some chefs are just better than others. Explore your dining options and try out new places. You may not only find better food, you may also find new friends along the way. Find out where the nearest grocery store and pizza delivery place are as well; at some point you may want a break from the dorm food.

Many school events like department socials, club meetings, and guest speaker lectures feature free food (the ethical bribe for attendance). This is a good chance to snack, and maybe learn something useful at the same time.

Explore off-campus offerings as well. In addition to your local pizza delivery, there are almost always restaurants just off-campus to take advantage of the ever-hungry student crowds. These are often cheap, quick eats, many of which may offer student discounts.

Be Resourceful About Resources

It bears repeating: Review your college website, scour the orientation materials, and call the administration offices in advance to become aware of all the services your school has to offer.

Colleges enhance their support services all the time, and a shockingly small number of students are even aware of what is available. If you know what's there for you, you'll be able to access the resource you need, if and when you need it. Become familiar with all of the tools and support your school offers and you will be ahead of the pack.

CHALLENGE # 10: ORIENTATION EXPLORATION

In addition to going to your school's orientation events, during your first few weeks of school and before your coursework becomes too intense, explore your new environment:

- Get a map of campus and walk around. See which buildings house which student services: the administration office, tutoring support, financial aid, medical services and the like. Locate your classes and time the walking (or bike riding) distance in between them.

- If your campus has a shuttle bus, take it for a ride and see where the stops are. Get a bus schedule and see what is available on the routes both on and off-campus.

- Find out where the nearby groceries, pharmacies, and other useful stores are.

- Check out whether there are hiking or biking trails on or near campus. See what attractions are nearby (museums, theaters, tourist destinations and other points of interest).

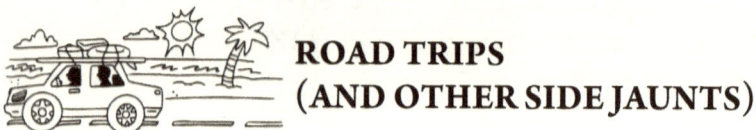

ROAD TRIPS (AND OTHER SIDE JAUNTS)

"Nothing is more expensive than a missed opportunity."
—H. Jackson Brown, Jr.

Once you are familiar with the regular academic road, you may find that you want to explore some side paths of particular interest, or blaze your own trail entirely. Maybe you want to add a certificate or minor to your curriculum, if your school offers that. Perhaps you'll want to combine two areas of focus and create your own independent study. Many colleges will allow you to combine subjects, if you work with your academic counselor early enough. If you wish to pursue your own path, make sure you understand what it takes within the system, and work with your counselor and the administration office to make it happen.

The World Beyond Your Doorstep

Some students burrow in and never stray beyond the path to their classes, dining hall, and dorm. Don't do this! There is a world to explore on campus, and even beyond. Before your coursework becomes too intense, take time to expand the broader geographic environment. There will be times when you'll need a mental break. It is useful to know your options for when you need a change of scene.

Check out other dorms, departments, campuses, and the cities that surround your campus. Look for opportunities to join or create a road trip to see a show, go shopping, watch a game, take a hike, hit the beach, all away from the four walls of your routine. Some colleges have clubs that arrange ski or beach trips, or offer sailing lessons, or other planned excursions during the term or spring break. Explore the possibilities and take advantage of them. Bake regular breaks into your schedule. It will let you give your mind a rest, refresh your spirit, and may even help you gain (or change) your perspective.

 **SAFETY CHECK**

If you are making the most of your journey, you will be exploring new ground. New people and places are waiting to be discovered. But to keep this adventure awesome, you will want to take a few precautions. Not everyone you meet will share your values, so consider a few safety tips, and make up your own that work best for you:

If you are hosting a big group in your room, lock up your valuables. Jewelry, cameras, laptop, cellphone (if it isn't on you), wallet, watch. Anything that you would hate to lose, take steps to protect.

If your dorm is hosting a big party open to outsiders, make sure that your room is locked. And lock up your valuables before you go.

If you are attending a party on campus, arrange to go with a friend and agree to a check- in plan to make sure everything stays okay. Maybe share your location with a select group of close friends. Plan your response to peer pressure in advance and know your limits before you go.

Don't leave open drinks unattended and don't drink anything that you haven't watched being poured. Binge drinking is dangerous: Alcohol poisoning is a real thing and students die of it. Don't let that be you.

It may sound trite, but "recreational" drugs are NEVER the right answer, and truly dangerous on so many levels. Seriously. Just don't.

If you are going off campus with someone, let a friend know where you are going, with whom, and when you expect to return. Check in if those plans change.

Use your campus resources to help you if you have questions or safety concerns, to bounce ideas off of, to cover physical health or mental health issues. Safety first!

Conclusion

Free yourself to wander. Around campus, off campus, through various class offerings. Remember that sometimes life's best experiences come from the unexpected paths. As long as you have your goals and ultimate destination mapped, you will have a good idea of when and how far you can take those side trips.

Remember Jean-Carlos? When the show was over and it was time for Jean-Carlos to meet up with his group at the international dorm, he still had no idea where he was, so he took a cab. During the long and convoluted ride back, Jean-Carlos reflected on his awesome day. Although he didn't make it to the museum he had intended to see, he'd had an amazing experience that he never would have planned for himself. He experienced universal emotions and audience reactions expressed in a language he didn't understand, in an entirely unexpected way. By getting lost, he found himself more comfortable with his decisions to explore new experiences. It reinforced to Jean-Carlos that sometimes you choose the road, but sometimes the road chooses you.

When you are lost or you find yourself off your planned route, take stock of your skills and center yourself. Keep an open mind. If you are willing to try new things, amazing experiences can be found.

 **KEY TIPS**

- USE ORIENTATION AND OTHER EVENTS ORGA-NIZED BY YOUR COLLEGE TO GET ACQUAINTED WITH THE CAMPUS, YOUR DEPARTMENT, AND ALL RESOURCES AVAILABLE TO YOU. DON'T FORGET THE STUDENT UNION, BOOKSTORE, FINANCIAL AID, TUTORING, AND OTHER PLANNED EVENTS.

- TAKE ADVANTAGE OF ESTABLISHED COLLEGE SYSTEMS: STUDENT COMMUNICATIONS FORUMS, SUPPORT, ON-CAMPUS JOBS, AND OTHER RESOURCES.

- BE OPEN TO NEW OPPORTUNITIES! EXPLORE BEYOND YOUR DORM, DINING HALL, AND CAMPUS TO TAKE A BREAK AND GAIN PERSPECTIVE.

Chapter 5

FINDING FELLOW TRAVELERS GOING YOUR WAY

"Whether you think you CAN, or you think you CAN'T—you're right."
—Henry Ford

It wasn't THE BIG GAME, which would occur later in the fall against the dreaded cross-town rivals. But it was A Big Game, against the hated football powerhouse in their division. Tyrone's school was the thirty-one-point underdog. It wasn't that their team was bad. Well, okay, they could be pretty bad. Every once in a while, though, they could be great. Inconsistent enough to keep hope alive, and expectations low.

It was a beautiful late September weekend, early enough in the quarter that midterms seemed light years away. Tyrone had been a little nervous about meeting people; he was shy and a bit awkward socially. The school was big and the freshman class filled with people who seemed to have it all together.

Not at all how Tyrone was feeling. But Tyrone was an avid football fan, so he got permission from his folks, then gathered his courage and reached out to some of his new dormmates, and some new acquaintances and some friends of friends, and invited them all on a road trip to support the team.

A caravan consisting of thirty-eight of Tyrone's new friends and acquaintances ultimately arrived at his parents' house, which was close enough to the rival stadium to use as home base. Space was cleared for sleeping bags and people were crammed into every available space. No one got much sleep, at least not the first night. They played music and games, laughed and sang and talked into the next day, when they left early to tailgate at the stadium.... .

GROWING YOUR GROUP: ACTION CREATES ATTRACTION

Whether it hits you at "goodbye" or a few weeks later, leaving home is harder than you may think. Let's be clear: You will be lonely at some point—whether it happens in your first week, or later, it will happen sometime. It can be hard to adjust to not having your family and friends immediately on hand.

Many students feel lonely shortly after they arrive on campus; those first few hours can be a little rough. Everyone is busy moving in, laughing, chattering together, and it is easy to feel alienated and already a bit defeated. Resist letting these feelings take hold and DO something about it right away. Wander down the hall to see if anyone needs help moving in, or open your door to invite visitors. A friendly face and open vibe will do wonders. It is normal to be a bit anxious, but don't let this overwhelm or stifle you. Remember: EVERYONE is new to this.

Throughout the first couple of weeks, take advantage of the orientation activities and meet as many people as you can. Where and when else will you find a group of people as new to an experience as you? Say hi to a stranger, go get dinner with random people from your dorm, include others, and attend as many events as you can. Remember that many people will feel as awkward and nervous as you are, so be courageous and take the first step. Make that good first impression.

Don't be discouraged if other people seem to have found their group right off the bat. No matter what it looks like, the people who seem like instant BFFs the first week don't always stay that way through their college years (although some do). People who you don't connect with right away can sometimes become some of your best friends. Be open and friendly, and see what happens from there.

Sometimes it takes a while to find your people. Be patient if it doesn't happen right away. It will happen if you continue to put yourself out there, especially after the first few weeks give way and people settle down into their new routines. Talk to people in your dorm, in the halls, or in the dining rooms. Talk to people while doing laundry.

Although a few people may have friends from home going to the same college, most people won't have anyone. Even those who do have high school friends may find that the friendship changes over time. You will never have as great an opportunity to get to know so many people on such a level playing field. So put yourself out there. **What you do (or don't do) will make all the difference over time.** You never know where it may lead.

Think of your first semester as a time to grow your potential group of friends. You want to be as open to meeting as many people as possible. Cast a broad net. Don't settle down too fast with the first few friends you meet and don't let the people you meet in the first few days limit the rest of your year. You will have a lot of opportunities to get to know a lot of people. Get out there and do it! Over time, you may find that the people you chose to share your college journey will narrow down to a number and level of engagement that suits you best.

 **HOW DO YOU START A CONVERSATION WITH PEOPLE YOU DON'T KNOW?**

Almost everyone feels awkward when first meeting people. In the age of social media, meeting people in real life can be even more challenging for those who are out of practice or shy. Even those who seem like the life of the party may have hidden doubts and insecurities. Freshman orientation is the perfect time to set the tone and to practice making friends, but you should continue this practice throughout your college years.

So how do you start? Try it old school. Dale Carnegie, in his classic book *How to Win Friends and Influence People*, says to get into the habit of looking for things you like and admire in the people you meet. But don't build up a whole scenario in your mind in advance. Enter conversations with no expectations, no prejudgments, and no pressure to reach any particular outcome.

Do's:

- Make eye contact and offer a smile. If it is returned, start by saying "hi" and introducing yourself.

- Offer a comment relating to the current circumstances: the difficulty in parking, the crowded lines at registration, the weather… whatever is going on around you, make it a shared experience. Turn the everyday into an observation you can briefly comment on, and if possible add a question at the end. For example, if someone has a book in their hand, you can ask, "How do you like that book?" Or if you share a class, ask how they like the professor. Maybe something like, "It feels like I haven't seen the sun in a month! How are you dealing with this rain?" or, "I always have trouble parking. Do you have any tips?" or, "I haven't had the chance to try the cafeterias in any of the other buildings, have you?" Simple niceties can build into more fulfilling conversations and friendships in time.

- Compliments can be appreciated, but be careful that they are authentic and aren't too personal. No girl wants the creepy stranger complimenting her on her nice...whatever. If someone made a good comment in class, reach out to them and say so. Your kindness will make them feel good, and you have a great conversation starter. Talking about subjects covered in a class is an easy ice breaker. Include others in the conversation, and your circle expands.

- Be curious and ask open-ended questions.

- Really listen to what others say and respond to them with genuine interest.

Don'ts:

- Too close, too exuberant, too loud, or too long is TOO MUCH right off the bat. You need to be aware of the response of the person with whom you want to engage. Sometimes when people are nervous, they tend to overshare. Try not to do this! Tone it down and let things develop at their own pace. And if you are on the receiving end of an overshare, remember that the person may just be nervous, so don't judge too harshly.

- Don't take a frosty response personally. It may be that the person is having a bad day. Or dealing with something completely unrelated to you. Be gracious in retreat. Evaluate the encounter: Is there something you did or could have done differently to be more successful? Learn clues from social cues, but don't let it stop you from approaching someone else.

TAKING AN
ENVIRONMENTAL APPROACH

Have you ever noticed that video games become more fun when they are multiplayer? That the play or film or concert is more enjoyable when you experience it with friends and discuss it together afterward? Your experience will be enhanced if you share your journey.

In college, you will be one who makes that happen. Be aware of events and activities going on in your dorm, in clubs, and on campus; take note of what interests you. Then whether it is reaching out to other people to invite them along or being open to others when they invite you, get out there! You will have the opportunity to choose how, when, and how deeply you want to get involved. Whether it is as friendly acquaintances or more, get to know the people around you.

Learn to develop relationships with people. From those who you smile at when you pass on the way to class, to those deeply trusted to whom you can reach out in good times and bad; from those who can help you with that problem set, to those with whom you share a laugh and plot adventures—forming and building relationships is an important skill. It takes practice. It can feel awkward at times. But the more you do this, the better you will become. You have a strong hand in determining your environment. Don't hide away in your dorm room playing videos or surfing social media. Make the decision to live in the real world. Invite people in; join them too. Make your world one in which you want to live.

You will be confronting a wide world of choices, and maybe for the first time, you'll be making some major decisions about your life and how to live it. Have your personal framework, values, and goals firmly in mind as you evaluate your options:

- To Greek or not to Greek?

- Which of the many clubs, groups, and choices best serve and support your goals?

- Are you outgoing and need people to help get and keep you motivated to buckle down and study? Or are you more of an introvert who needs someone to get you out of your shell?

- Do you need someone to balance your natural tendencies? Or to strengthen those traits you want to enhance?

You can reinforce your willpower with the power of like-minded people. Knowing yourself and having clarity around what serves your goals will help cull the herd. Have study buddies as well as party buddies. Have people to work out with as well as chill out with. Think about the environment you want to create for yourself as you meet and grow your social network.

Explore clubs, music, intramural sports, whatever fills you with joy. In the first few days especially, but throughout your college journey, look to find ways to meet, connect, support (and be supported by) your fellow travelers. Put the FUN into building a wide funnel of friends. Use the resources available to you. And don't forget the physical bits.

Above all, be proactive! If there isn't a club or group that does what you're most excited about, check with the Student Union and see if you can create one. Many schools have a budget for student groups. I've heard of a bagel eating club that met once a week to sample different bagels, food truck afficionados who tried out a new food truck once a month, film clubs that watched a movie once a week, and hiking groups that explored trails. Anything that brings like-minded people together, for learning or just for fun, is worth pursuing.

CHALLENGE # 11: FIND YOUR PEOPLE

Plan how you will approach setting up your social environment:

- Make a list of your hobbies, interests, and values that are important to you. Include things you have enjoyed in the past, as well as those you'd like to explore:

  o Do you love to play jazz or ultimate frisbee? Enjoy theater? Gaming? Writing for the school paper? Making films? Do you want to learn to swim? Or knit? There may be clubs for that, or you can start your own.

  o Are you passionate about the environment or politics? Performing charitable or community good works? Are you spiritual or religious? There likely will be organized groups or events in which you can participate.

  o What about affinity groups? There may be groups dedicated to special interests like LGBTQ+, Black Student Union, Mexican Heritage, etc.

- Now brainstorm how you might meet people who share these interests with you.

  o Are you taking classes in this arena? What will you do to meet classmates?

  o Are there existing clubs for this hobby?

  o Are there affinity groups for students who share your heritage or orientation?

  o Do any of your dormmates share your interests? If so, can you come up with ideas together?

o   Does your college have a subreddit or Instagram to make connections?

By identifying those activities that bring you joy, you have a great place to start to find your tribe.

Outline your plan and the steps you can take to meet people who share your hobbies, interests, and values, then put your plan into action.

Create challenges for yourself: For example, to say hi to five people, to comment on a class to three people a week, to form a group to go hiking within the first month, to ask someone to meet for coffee, to chose a different study space each week for a month, or any other action that will put you out there to connect in real life. Write your challenges down in your planner and commit to completing at least one challenge a week. Stretch yourself, and notice that what is so hard to do when you start becomes so much easier the more you practice.

Remember that everyone wants to fit in. If you take the first step, you will make it easier for someone else. Balance the brief discomfort of making the effort against the loneliness and isolation that could occur if you don't—and then choose to take the risk. Develop the habit of meeting people, not just at the beginning, but throughout your college journey, and your experience will be richer for it.

Party and Other Peer Pressure

You've probably heard stories of wild times, out-of-control drinking and drugs at college. Free from parental control and oversight, some students go a little crazy. Some use this time to test their boundaries. Some use drinking or drugs to escape pressure. Some party to loosen up and relax. Whatever the reason, you likely will have the opportunity and maybe even feel pressured to "party." Remember always that you have the power to choose how to respond.

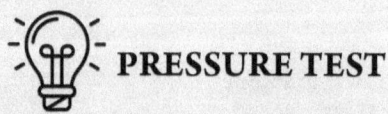 **PRESSURE TEST**

"Get Along," "Go Along," or "Move Along" is a framework of some choices to consider when confronting pressure to party, or any other peer pressure, for that matter. Using the party example:

- *Get Along.* Maybe you know that this type of party simply isn't your scene. You don't have to go to the party at all, if you don't want to. You can choose not to associate the people involved altogether. Or you can choose to say no to the party but remain friends with the people who do go. You can relive the exploits by talking to people who were there. If you express an interest in what happened later and can listen without judgment, you can get along with the partiers and find other things in common. You don't have to go along to get along!

- *Go Along.* Maybe you feel like you'd be missing out if you don't go to the party. So go! You still have control about how you act while you're there. You don't have to drink so much that you make yourself sick or drink yourself into oblivion. You don't have to drink at all! If you feel out of place, you can take one drink cup and hold onto it all night. You can circulate through the party or hang at the edges. You can decide how to make your own fun. For example, you can find a partner to do the drinking on your behalf while you play beer pong. At all times it is up to you decide how far you want to go along.

- **Move Along.** You may go to a party that starts out fun, but then careens out of control. Don't stay—especially if you can see that the situation is becoming dangerous! Call a sober driver if you've been drinking. Remember that your ability to assess your capacity is impaired if you've been indulging, and decide before you go to the party what your exit plan will be. Along the way, you may meet people who your intuition tells you are just trouble. Move along and stay away. You will find other people who are your people.

Whether it is pressure to party or other peer pressure, learning how to manage these types of pressures is a key part of being an adult. In your college years, you likely will confront some major decisions: about sex, alcohol, drugs, what to share on social media, how you will respond to peer pressure. Stay true to yourself, use your college resources for advice and help if you need it, and learn as you go. You alone will make your decisions, but you don't need to make your decisions alone! Use your personal goals and values to guide you as you make your decisions, and keep safety in mind. You don't want to make your learning curve too costly if you can avoid it. If you do make a choice you later regret, don't dwell on the mistake. Learn from it and resolve to make a better decision the next time.

Living on Your Own

A big part of freshman year is about learning how to live on your own for the first time. How to do your own laundry, how to wake up at 8 a.m. for class, how to feed yourself, and for some, how to drink responsibly. Success in freshman year is half about being a good student, going to class consistently, writing papers, studying effectively, and meeting deadlines. The other half is learning how to take care of yourself and live with other people from diverse backgrounds and with different values. Learning how to integrate both halves will give you valuable life skills that will serve you well after graduation.

After all the anticipation of finally being able to live on your own, you may be shocked to learn that you really aren't completely on your own after all. Although some may have a single room or apartment, very few freshmen live entirely on their own. If not roommates, there are floormates, dormmates, apartment mates that share your living space, common areas, dining halls, kitchen, laundry room, library, and fitness center. The good news: They'll be there with, and sometimes for, you. The bad news: Sometimes it may be hard to get away from them.

Roommate Etiquette

Have you heard the one about the guy who had the nerve to pound on his dormmate's door at 3 a.m.? Seriously, 3 a.m.! Luckily the dormmate was already awake playing bagpipes at the time....

Okay, the likelihood that someone will be practicing bagpipes in your dorm may be slim. But there will be other provocations, for sure. Freshman year is about how to deal with annoying roommates or others in your dorm, on your floor, in your room. Everyone's heard the nightmare stories of the roommates from hell: the one who's up all partying all night while you're trying to sleep, the one who sleeps all day so you don't have any time to yourself in the room, the one who's a total slob, the one who leaves food out and attracts all manner of bugs, or the one who refuses to bathe or use deodorant so that even the strongest Febreze is no match.

We don't all come to college with the same background. This is great for diversity of opinions and growth, but you may find it shocking how much you assume things because of your family background and upbringing. Some people have grown up in big families who have strict rules about sharing (or no rules at all, and whoever grabs first wins). Some people were only children who have never had to share anything at all. There are those who have been raised to believe that it is rude to argue, and there are those who have grown up learning that the way to express respect is to argue every little thing. Until you live with someone who has not grown up in your family, community, or geography, you may not realize how much of what you think is "normal" behavior has been shaped by your past and may not seem normal to someone else. Your unique upbringing has conditioned your unique values, judgments, and assumptions.

Learning to live with a diverse group of people can be difficult at first, but it is a huge opportunity for you to grow and enhance your understanding, not just of others, but of yourself as well. Communication is key. In the first few days, have a conversation with your roommate about non-negotiables, preferences, etc. Respectful but clear, open, and proactive communications are critical. Discuss issues when they first arise, before they become too emotionally charged. Look for solutions together.

When you have a failure to communicate and you just can't resolve a conflict, use the resources your college has: Some will allow you to switch roommates as a last resort; some will have an RA intervention. Try to view the experience as one that will give you stories to laugh at later. Sometimes you may find that the irritating creature with whom you've been stuck will teach you something you need to know about yourself and help you change for the better. Maybe they will become your best friend in the end … or maybe not.

Living Off Campus

Some students will live off campus, with their families, with other students, or even alone. If this is you, you will want to make an effort to integrate yourself into the fabric of your university. In addition to blocking out the extra time commuting, look for ways to optimize the time you spend on campus. Pay close attention to upcoming events, find a close friend who can invite you to open dorm activities, join a club or affinity group to keep you involved. If possible and economically viable, see if finding a job on campus makes sense for you.

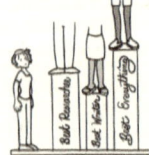 ## COMPARISON DROPPING

Have you ever felt like everywhere you look, it seems that EVERYONE else is having a better life? More friends, more fun, more achievements, more awards, better grades, more travel, more money, more, more, more.

One of the hardest things to do is to keep your eyes on your own road and not track everyone else's progress. As difficult as it may be, try not to compare yourself to others. With all the social media platforms, and gossip being what it is, there will be ample opportunities to look at what or how other people are doing—or how they want you to *think* they're doing. Resist this! Although "everyone else" may look like they are perfect, they aren't. You KNOW this. People post doctored pictures, make up stories, and leave out what they don't want you to know about. Don't let this derail you from YOUR path and what you want to accomplish.

Everyone has their own struggles, challenges, and obstacles to overcome. Some may do this with outward ease, but this doesn't mean that they don't have difficulties. "Effortless perfection" is a myth, and a very dangerous one at that. When people feel that they have to present themselves as perfect, they isolate themselves. They build walls behind the fake personas and miss out on the opportunity to really connect with others. They don't reach out for help if they need it. It is easy for them to become lonely and depressed, missing out on authentic relationships. And it is exhausting trying to be perfect all the time.

And it sets up a bad comparison. It can make other people feel like failures and give up. Which means they miss out on the chance to grow and they feel bad on top of it. Don't buy into this false belief. You are NOT a failure if you are not perfect, or if things are difficult for you. Growth and learning take work. Sometimes hard work. But it is through the struggle that real growth and mastery occurs.

The only person that you need to compare yourself to is ... YOURSELF. Not how you "should" be, but how you are. Track your own progress and compare how you are today against how you were yesterday, last week, last month, last year. Have you improved? Learned? Grown? Added skills? Gained confidence, wisdom, battle scars? Take a moment to appreciate your accomplishments, and let that momentum fuel your forward progress.

Whenever you're in doubt, go back to your list of strengths. You belong here and you are worthy! If you see people who seem more confident, self-assured, smart, whatever, remember that you are only seeing the outside persona and you don't know the whole picture. Try to be happy for the successes of your peers and continue on your own road. Let your "why" guide you and work on being the best YOU that you can be.

No one is perfect. Period. But even if they were—they are not on YOUR journey. Remember the strengths you packed as you started out. Those are still your strengths, in a combination that is uniquely you, and you may already have gained new ones. You are the only one on your personal journey and no one can compare exactly with you. Be the hero of your own story. Focus on your true north, plan your itinerary, work hard and continue forward step by step. You will make the progress you need to get to your destination.

Conclusion

Remember Tyrone? Going to the game was fun, but even better was the experience the group shared.

Tyrone and each of his now new friends left with memories, stories to tell, and new or deepened relationships.

It also started a tradition: the next year, when their school's team played against another rival, people in the group reached out to Tyrone and asked if they were going to do it again. And they did, every year for the four years he was in college. People in other dorms heard of their adventure and were inspired to organize their own road trips. Tyrone heard that the RAs in the dorm recruited other students to keep the tradition alive even after they graduated.

This never would have happened if Tyrone had been afraid to take the chance and reach out. If he had been concerned that parents' house wasn't the biggest or grandest. If he had thought that people would be judgmental that they had to bring sleeping bags and sleep on the floor. In truth, none of his fears were justified. Everyone who went treasured the memories and was thankful to have been included. He didn't really know any of those people at first. But he took the risk to have an adventure. And because he did, he made new friends, found friends for others, and created lasting memories. He started a trend and left a legacy.

Imagine what can happen if YOU take a chance? Put yourself out there and find your people. It will make all the difference, to you and to them.

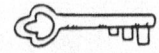 **KEY TIPS**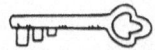

- BRAINSTORM IDEAS TO FIND YOUR PEOPLE IN ADVANCE, CASTING THE BROADEST NET POSSIBLE. CHALLENGE YOURSELF TO TAKE ACTION ON YOUR IDEAS.

- TAKE RESPONSIBILITY FOR CREATING YOUR ENVIRONMENT: FIND FRIENDS, SPACES, PLACES, AND SYSTEMS THAT WILL SUPPORT YOUR JOURNEY, SAFEGUARD YOUR SUCCESS, AND PROPEL YOU TO REACH YOUR DESTINATION.

- REMEMBER THAT YOUR JOURNEY IS UNIQUELY YOURS. DON'T BE DISTRACTED BY OTHERS' SUCCESS. USE IT AS A BEACON AS TO WHAT'S POSSIBLE, BUT KEEP PROGRESSING ON YOUR PATH.

Chapter 6

HABITS TO TURBOCHARGE YOUR ADVENTURE

"You cannot escape the responsibility of tomorrow by evading it today."
—Abraham Lincoln

Andrew dodged the frisbee his roommate Jackson flung at him. "Come on, Andrew. We need you on our team, and your paper isn't due until next week," Jackson taunted. Andrew shook his head. "Can't," he said. "I'm meeting my study group for coffee in an hour, and I have to get my research sites logged before then." Jackson, who had coasted through with straight As in high school, shook his head. Why would anyone study so hard? He chuckled, then ran out to join the pick-up volleyball game.

Andrew watched him go and, for a moment, felt a little low. He wished he could be as carefree as Jackson. He wished that things would come a little more easily for him. Andrew had been born with some learning challenges, and school had never been easy for him. But Andrew had been determined to make it into this university. He had been forced to learn study skills that worked for him. He knew when his focus was sharpest and that he needed regular breaks to refresh himself. He knew how to estimate how long it would take to do assignments and to leave room for extra time.

Andrew thought about a conversation he'd had just that afternoon with Olivia, another dormmate that he had seen around, but didn't know well. Andrew had run into her at the laundromat and was surprised to see her crying. Olivia had always been composed and calm, and seeing her so upset seemed really out of character. She shared that she had received her first test scores, and she had bombed. She had never failed a test before and she didn't know what to do. She was afraid to call her parents. She didn't want anyone to think she couldn't cut it, but her confidence was shattered. Andrew could tell she was panicked and depressed.

"Look," Andrew had said, "no one is going to judge you. And even if they do, that's their issue, not yours. The important thing is not that you failed this test. The important thing is what you learn from it, and what you're going to do about it next. It's early in the semester. You have time to recover. But whatever you do, you shouldn't hide from it, or ignore it. That will only make things worse.

"What do you think went wrong?" Andrew asked.

Olivia thought about it for a few minutes. "Well," she said, "I think I started studying for the test too late. Tests have always been easy for me in the past, and I underestimated the amount of material that we'd covered." She thought some more. "I didn't review the material as I went along," she continued. "I just finished the assignments and moved on. And I'm not sure that I focused on the right points to study. Some of the questions seemed so obscure!"

"I know some people who are taking that class," Andrew said. "I'd be happy to introduce you to them so you can see if they want to form a study group. You might also want to see your professor during his next office hours, go over your test and see why you missed the main points. He might have some suggestions about how you can study better."

Olivia took a deep breath. Not a smile yet, but Andrew could see that she was now thinking about how to move forward and create some new study patterns. "Thank you, Andrew. It's been really helpful talking to you."

"It's always better to talk to someone, Olivia. There is always someone who can help, if we just reach out. We're all in this together." Andrew left the laundromat feeling that he had formed a new friendship and thankful that could help a fellow student.

Maybe the fact that Andrew had had to overcome learning challenges and mastered strong study skills was a benefit after all, he mused. Feeling slightly better, Andrew looked down at his paper, and got back to work.

When you first started school, your first main task was to learn to read. As you moved up the grades, the task changed from learning to read to reading to learn. As you step up to college, your task changes again. Now you'll be tasked with learning how to learn, how to use critical thinking about what you learn, and how to extend that knowledge to another level.

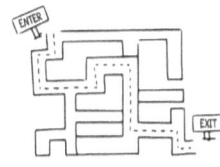 ## BEYOND EFFORT TO EFFECTIVE: ACCELERATE YOUR RESULTS

It's not the same old game. Do you know that saying that if you keep doing what you have done, you will get the same results? Well, this isn't entirely true when it comes to transitioning from high school to college. One thing that is absolutely sure: Your college experience will be very different from the one you had in high school. What got you here may not be sufficient to keep you here. In college, you may need to elevate your game just to stay on the field, much less win the game.

For example, you may have been able to get by in high school with superficial memorizing, but that will no longer work in college. You may have been able to get good grades by just repeating what your teacher said, but that may not be enough now. You may have been able to wait until the night before to study for your tests, or write your paper, or pull together your project. No more! This journey requires a whole new level of effort on your part.

Merely knowing what to do isn't enough. How you choose to approach your journey, what you learn about yourself along the way, and discovering and adapting to how you learn best, all will shape your college experience. You have to take ACTION to make success happen. Remind yourself of your "why" and resolve to make positive progress: consistently, intentionally, resiliently. Make the effort to learn and improve every day.

However, effort alone will not suffice. Not if you truly want to get the most out of your college education. Remember, **this isn't just about grades, it's about what this adventure will set you up to achieve**. The skills you'll master, the deeper understanding you will gain, the way you position yourself for future challenges: all of these matter. This means that it is no longer just about the *effort* you put in, but the *results* you achieve when you set yourself up for success.

Beware the Buffet

> *"You CAN have it all. Just not all at once."*
> —Oprah Winfrey

Have you ever been to an "all you can eat" buffet? Tempted by so many mouth-watering choices, you pile your plate with everything on offer… and end up with a huge stomachache from overeating. This same problem can occur when you set out to embrace all of the wonderful options available to you at college all at once. In your excitement, you want to do EVERYTHING. Although there is nothing wrong with that spirit, it is critical to know that while you may be able to do everything you want OVER TIME, you can't do everything all at once.

Overcommitting out of the gate—to classes, social clubs, dorm activities and the like—is a sure recipe for stress and burnout. Even if you manage to survive the multiple demands, you won't be able to do your best in them.

You've surveyed all of the alternatives available to you. Now you need to think about the time and resource commitments your choices require, and choose wisely, in line with your priorities. Maybe you will choose to put off joining that club this semester. Or maybe choose to join but don't take on a leadership role this time. If you plan ahead and take into account the cumulative effect of your activities, you can get the most out of your involvement.

A Simple Approach

One simple approach to succeed in college academically is this:

- Attend and actively listen in class.

- Take notes on the lectures and readings.

- Review your notes shortly after making them to anchor in your learning.

- Keep up with the pace of the class (don't fall behind).

- Learn each class's material as if you had to teach it to next year's class.

There are several ways to learn as if you're going to teach: Go over your notes and translate them into your own words. Confirm your understanding with the professor or TA during office hours. Review your notes while you're exercising. Discuss them with a classmate or study group, or explain them to a willing listener. Take the time and put in the effort to discover the methods that work best for you—and make those methods your habit.

Most importantly, find the JOY—in the class, in the course, in connecting your class to your "why"—and use that joy to help you dive deeper into the material. Joyful learning lasts. If you can do this, you will succeed.

Below are some additional tips, tricks, and habits that you can adopt to ease your journey and increase the return on your efforts.

The Easy-Hard Paradox.

The easiest road may not always be the best in the long term, and, paradoxically, taking the harder road may actually get you to your destination more quickly. Put another way, the right thing to do may sometimes be the hardest to do in the moment, but will pave an easier path in the longer run.

Forcing yourself to put away the game controller and pick up your book to study during the quarter may be difficult in the moment but will make studying for your finals easier. Passing up the brownie and choosing fruit may be tough in the moment but being fit can help your focus and make things easier for you in the longer term. Making yourself work out rather than vegging in front of the TV may be difficult, but the results can reduce stress and make your studying easier. Going to that extra lab rather than hanging with your friends may seem like a bummer, but that extra lab may be just the thing that has you ace the test. The small choices you make daily add up over time. If you make it a habit to choose the more difficult, more disciplined approach in your small daily choices, you will have an easier time in the end. Everyone wants to take it easy sometimes. But remember that the hardest route may pave the easiest way to the most rewarding destination.

You can do hard things! And paradoxically, the more you do hard things, the easier it becomes to do them. Master the "easy-hard" paradox and you'll master your journey.

Make Study Your Buddy

Figure out how you work best as soon as you can. This will help you make the most of the time you spend studying.

Set up your environment to support your success. Block out time to study when your attention is strongest. Seek a place that minimizes distractions and strengthens your focus. Pay attention to whether you study best in your dorm room with earplugs, or at the library, or in a conference room. Find wherever works best for you and build a plan to go there, regularly. Join people who already are doing what you want to do; learn from their experience. Build routines to support your study. If you create the right environment, you will create a form of gravity to pull you toward your goals.

Make good habits easy and bad habits hard. Sometimes there is strength in numbers. If you can't focus on your own, leverage and lever up your tribe. Form a study group, if that works for you. Sometimes it does, sometimes it wastes time. You'll need to decide for yourself what works best for you and with whom you have the best study success.

Sometimes groups are too distracting and inefficient. In this case, you may want to find an accountability partner. An accountability partner is someone with whom you can work well, even if you are not working on the same thing, or even at the same time. It can be someone from your class, or your dorm, or anyone responsible who agrees to check in with you on progress and to keep each other on track.

SCHEDULE SUCCESS WITH YOUR SYLLABUS

"If you fail to plan, you are planning to fail."
—Ben Franklin

College freshmen often take a while to figure out that you can't regularly get away with last-minute cramming. If you ignore major papers or projects until the last minute, do not expect to do well. Even if you somehow do manage to get a decent grade, you will have cheated yourself out of the opportunity to do your best and really learn something, which wastes the time and money you are spending for this adventure.

Some people use the time stress to motivate themselves, thinking that they work best under pressure. Although it is true that time pressure can add focus, it does not lead to doing your best work. And when you remember what YOU want to accomplish on your journey and your "why," this is probably not your best technique.

So what can you do? Often by the first week of each class, you will be given a syllabus. This will include the key projects, papers, homework exercises, big assignments, mid-term exams, and finals, and when they are due. Take the time right away to write these deadlines in your calendar. Then schedule time to work on each project. So, for example: If you have a large research paper due in three weeks, book blocks of time now to begin working on it. If you have a group project due in two weeks, meet with your group immediately to book time together to work on it; assign responsibilities and schedule check-ins to ensure that everyone is accountable and doing what they need to do. Extra points if you put SMART goals for the time that you book! (More about SMART goals later).

Remember: You can do almost anything, but not everything (at least not all at once). Once you get in the habit of calendaring your time to work on each of your assignments, you will smooth out your workload, avoid unnecessary stress and regret, and put yourself in a strong position to succeed.

Can You Calendar It?

College is a great time to build a habit of using a calendar or planner, if you don't have one already. It can be a paper calendar, an online calendar, a whiteboard on your wall, or even the calendar on your phone. The point is to use one single spot as the place where you list deadlines (when something has to be done and submitted) and commitments (where you have to be when). It will let you plan your workload, balance your social life, and keep you on track. It can provide a visual point of reference and offer reminders. It is also a great place to capture random thoughts and ideas that pop up. Rather than let those ideas slip away or distract you from your task at hand, drop them into your planner or in notes on your cellphone for later action.

Registration is one example of how calendaring sets you up for success. If class registration is competitive at your school, you'll want to note the first day (and maybe even time!) you're eligible to register. Let's say that all 1000 freshmen have to take "College Writing 101" but there are only ten sections with eighty spots each offered first semester. One student has "first day to obtain a registration appointment" marked on their calendar, with the start time noted and a reminder set in their phone; another student only has the entry "deadline to register for classes" on their calendar; and a third student has no entry at all. Who do you think is going to have a better chance to get one of those 800 spots in the writing class, and on the day and time they want it? Use your calendar to schedule your time and plan your projects. Keep to your schedule and watch as your productivity explodes!

Don't spend too much time getting ready to get ready. Take immediate action, even if only in small steps. Rather than add another item to your to-do list, why not just send that email, or book that appointment, or jot down those class note right now? Grab people on your group project immediately after class and pull out schedules right away, rather than spend more time later as everyone tries to coordinate via text or email to find a time that works for all. When you have good habits, time works for you; when you have bad habits, time works against you. Make it a habit to take action right away if you can.

Make sure that you aren't using time as an excuse to procrastinate. Don't put off tasks thinking that you need a solid block of time to get started. Jump in! Use the small time blocks to review your schedule, knock out quick assignments, or take steps towards a bigger assignment. Don't fritter away time in which you can make progress. Use small time blocks to build momentum.

Keep Your Own Score Right From the Start

Another big difference between high school and college is that no one is keeping score but you. Before you got to college, you may have had other people constantly giving you feedback and monitoring whether you were on track. You may have had people jumping in if you were missing the main points of the lessons or falling behind. You may have had people praising you for your efforts or progress. You may have had people checking to make sure you did your homework or studied for a test.

In college it is all up to you. There is great freedom in this, but it can be a shock to the system. Some students don't find out that they are in trouble until they fail their first midterm! Some students who have excelled at everything they tried in high school will find that some courses don't come as easily to them in college. Unlike high school, not all college courses have graded homework. This means that you won't have the same amount of feedback that you have had in high school. You won't necessarily know that you've missed the point, or gotten off track, until it may be too late. **You need to be your own monitor and put a plan in place to track your own progress.**

How can you do this? What if you're in a class that doesn't have any grading until the midterm? First, try not to fall behind on the assignments. Don't just speed read through the material. Take notes in class and on the readings, and really make sure you understand what's being covered. (Bonus if you figure out *why* the material is included in the class—that can really deepen your learning). Get together with others in your class and discuss the material. Take advantage of your professor or TAs' office hours to confirm that you're getting the main points.

Some classes will track attendance, but most won't. You get to choose whether you attend your classes or not, but know that your decision will have a direct effect on how much you get out of the class and how well you absorb the material. This, in turn, will have a strong correlation to how well you do on the final paper or exam. But the reality is that sometimes you're going to miss a class due to illness or other factors, and—newsflash—the world will continue to revolve.

It is the same thing with grades. Your transcript at the end of each semester won't be seen by anyone but you unless you show it to them. And unless you plan to apply to a competitive grad school immediately after graduation, the occasional poor grade won't stop your progress as long as you have sufficient passing grades and units to graduate.

Making the Grade

So why care about your grades anyway? They may set a guidepost for whether you truly understand and are mastering the material. This becomes important if you are presumed to have gained expertise in a subject post-graduation.

Good grades also demonstrate to future employers, partners, and affiliates that you were able to go the distance in the class: You didn't give up, you understood the assignments and materials, and you met (or exceeded) performance requirements. All of these characteristics signal that you are capable of succeeding in your post-college endeavors.

You may be asked to provide your transcript to a future employer, which may make a difference in whether you get an interview. Some schools require a certain GPA before you can declare certain majors. Position yourself for these opportunities by tracking your grades (as a reflection of your learning) and commit to doing your best right from the start.

If you DO plan to apply to a competitive graduate program right after graduation, the grades on your transcript may make a big difference, so you will need to pay additional attention to your performance. Students with graduate school ambitions tend to start monitoring their transcript and working toward getting A's early in their college career. In this case, the price of poor grades can be a little higher than in other circumstances and may require some additional planning and actions on your part to recover. You may need to retake classes, or take additional ones. You may need to design an alternative route to your destination: a gap year, maybe a master's degree prior to applying to med school, for example, or work experience, foreign schools, or some other approach, depending on your circumstances and goals. The big point to remember is that there are many paths up the mountain, and even if your grades cause a delay in your plans, you can find alternatives if you persevere.

If you receive a poor grade or two, resolve to learn from your mistakes and do better next time. You are learning in many dimensions in college: How to be on your own, how to self-initiate, how to learn in a new environment, and, of course, the material itself. It is a LOT to absorb! So give yourself a little leeway, and compassion if you don't get it right every time. Take your lumps, learn and grow, make the adjustments you need to, and get back on your path. Explore ways to recover from the stumbles. See if you can retake the class or add relevant work experience. Be able to explain what happened and what you learned from it in a way that shows your growth and maturity.

The bottom line: Do what you can to prepare to succeed, set up a plan to track your own progress, learn lessons from any falls along the way, and recover when you do. Shake off the missed shots and losses, learn your lessons, and come back strong.

Office Hours: Your Underused Superpower

Have you ever played a video game where there are hidden powers, secret passageways, or special weapons that you can find during the game? And if you collect these hidden powers, you can go further or faster or better as the game progresses? Well, you can have that in-college special boost in the form of your professors' office hours.

This is the easiest and one of the least used methods of making sure that you are on track. Gather your notes, be prepared to discuss the material, and go to the source. It is astounding how few students take advantage of this ready resource! It can be your secret superpower.

So why don't students take advantage of professor or TA office hours? Professors are leaders in their field and worthy of your respect, to be sure. But they are people, too. And although there are exceptions, many have a deep passion for their subject and want to pass that passion on to you!

Maybe you're afraid you'll look foolish or expose that you don't fully understand the material. Don't give in to this fear. Your tuition helps to pay their salary, and office hours are part of what you're paying for. Your professors are there to help you. They want you to learn. Help them help you. And which would you prefer: to save your pride but fail the course, or get the course correction help you need and succeed? It should be an easy choice. Get past your fear or embarrassment, choose to use this superpower, and you'll enrich both your knowledge and your college experience.

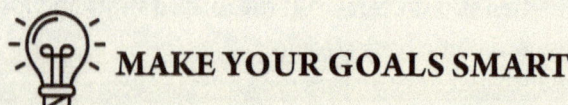 **MAKE YOUR GOALS SMART**

It has been said that a goal is a wish with a deadline. If you set a goal and work to achieve it, almost anything can be yours.

A "SMART" goal is a method to create a specific type of action plan to achieve results. To be SMART, your goal must be <u>Specific</u>, <u>Measurable</u>, <u>Actionable</u>, <u>Reasonable</u>, and <u>Time-based</u>. It breaks down your high-level wishes into a plan to take concrete steps toward, and ultimately achieve results. So how does this work for you?

- **Specific**: First, define each goal as clearly and specifically as you can. Take it down to the clearest, most basic steps. For example, rather than "Get an A in Comparative Lit," you might instead set a goal of "Review the notes for Comparative Lit once a week for no less than thirty minutes," or "Take no less than thirty minutes to rewrite notes for Comparative Lit on same day of each class," or "Set up study group for Comparative Lit to meet Monday and Wednesday for a half-hour each week to compare notes and discuss materials"—you get the picture. Your goals build to the "A" you seek, creating a series of specific steps that you can accomplish to take you there.

- **Measurable**: Make sure your success at the task is measurable. Is it something you can check off your to-do list when completed? Are there ways to measure that it has been done and done well?

- **Actionable**: Ensure that each goal has a specific action. Don't leave it vague or theoretical. Make sure it's something you can actually DO. For example, find five sources to place in the bibliography for your paper. Or complete five math problem sets by the end of the day. Meet with your study group for 30 minutes. The key is to choose an action that you can take.

- **Reasonable**: Ask yourself: Is this goal something I can reasonably accomplish based on the time, resources, and ability I have at my disposal? It's okay (and often great!) for a goal to be challenging, but be careful you're not setting up unrealistic expectations for yourself that will inevitably lead to disappointment.

- **Time-based**: Make sure you've set a time period in which you will perform each task, where there's a clear beginning and end. Leaving a task open-ended will just leave you frustrated.

Create your SMART goals for each semester and map them to your calendar schedule, check in on them to make sure you are keeping to them, and modify them as needed to address any additional challenges or obstacles that pop up along the way. You can't help but succeed!

Stack Habits to Make Incremental Progress (and Improvements)

There's an old saying, "What's hard by the yard is a cinch by the inch." Small, incremental steps are not just achievable, but the easiest way to make consistent, sustainable progress toward your goals.

Whether you have defined SMART goals for yourself or not, gaining the habit of making even small improvements **consistently** will aggregate up to major results over time. James Clear, in his blockbuster book *Atomic Habits*, sets the target to achieve a mere one percent better every day to create a habit of progress. That might translate to time: getting up and going one minute earlier, adding one more minute of exercise or one more minute of studying before picking up the remote to your video game. It might translate to effort: one more piece of research, one more proofread of your paper before you submit it, one more sit-up to strengthen your core. It could translate to expanding out of your comfort zone: challenging yourself to reach out to one more person to make a new friend, speaking out in one class a semester, then month, then week. Forward progress doesn't have to happen in huge leaps; it can happen in tiny steps taken each day.

An effective way to build consistency in your progress is to "stack habits." You stack habits by adding the new action to a routine you already have. For example, add five minutes of stretching right before (or right after) you brush your teeth every day. Or if you're trying to limit the time you spend on social media, perhaps allot yourself ten minutes only after you've eaten a meal. If you have a an evening routine, think about adding a new healthy process to it, such as listening to soothing music or a guided mediation before bedtime to train your body to transition to sleep. Or add a few minutes in the morning to review your schedule before you start your day. Set your new habits to your existing patterns, and they will be easier to adopt and maintain.

An Attitude of Latitude—But Practice with Precision

Once you've acquired a new skill, it's easy to forget how hard it was at the beginning. When you were learning to walk, you fell down quite a bit. It may have felt impossible at the time, but you were determined, and kept at it, and eventually learned to walk. Similarly, seemingly impenetrable math problems—like long division at first, and maybe algebra later—became easy once you figured them out. It may have taken time and multiple attempts, but you pushed through the frustration and got there. It's the same when you're learning to play a sport—there was a time when simply playing catch was a challenge. When you start learning to play a musical instrument even the simplest pieces can be challenging. All of these tasks may come naturally for you now, and you may now take your abilities for granted.

In college, some of your new tasks, courses, assignments, projects, and subjects may not be easy at first. But as with any new skill that must be learned, the more and better you practice, the better you will become at it. And as you increase your mastery, your capabilities will expand. You will gain strength and form a foundation upon which you can build even more difficult tasks.

But it didn't start out easy. It is CRITICAL to remember this, because you will be confronted with challenges in college that may require you to try and fail until you get it. You may be challenged to deepen your thinking, grapple with new concepts, or sharpen your critical thinking. You may be pressed to absorb material more quickly, to write more clearly, or to work through coding assignments or problem sets on stricter deadlines than you're used to. Just as you wouldn't expect to play a piano concerto in your first week of piano lessons, allow yourself time and trials to grow to mastery in your college courses. Give yourself the latitude to learn. Protect your confidence and remember that it is your progress, not perfection, that matters most as you challenge yourself to higher and higher achievements.

CHALLENGE # 12: YOU LEARNED THIS, TOO

Take a moment to brainstorm and write down things, large and small, that you are good at now that you weren't when you first tried them. If the examples don't come easy, keep at it, and you will find that the floodgates will eventually open. Give yourself at least fifteen minutes to collect and acknowledge your prior successes. Remember the frustration you might have felt when you first started out. How the task seemed so hard, and you wanted to give up, and you had to force yourself to push through. Then remember that amazing feeling when you made it! When you played that piano piece perfectly, or made the basket, or figured out the math problem, or made it to the top of the mountain, or skied down it. Keep this list handy and look at it when you feel stretched and stressed. You CAN do hard things. Sometimes you may simply need a reminder.

Don't expect to have everything go perfectly right out the gate, but don't give in to half-measured efforts. The correct rule isn't "practice makes perfect," rather it is "**perfect** practice makes perfect." If you try to shoot free throws that aren't going in, but don't make any corrections to your stance or how you hold the ball, you won't make any progress. Shooting the ball the same wrong way twenty times, or fifty times, or a hundred times isn't going to get you better at shooting free throws. The same with learning to play new musical pieces. You need to adjust until you can get it right consistently, then practice as perfectly as possible to build it into muscle memory. Once it's there, it becomes foundational, and a skill that you can carry onto the next part of your journey.

Don't be paralyzed by "Perfection"

Although you try to hit perfection in your practice, we humans are not perfect. Don't let your quest for perfection cause you to give up (or worse yet, fail to start) because you can't hit that unattainable goal. Rather, look at it as "perfect practice makes **progress**", and have that be your goal. As long as you are learning, improving and progressing, you are succeeding.

If you continue to try with your best efforts, make adjustments where needed to improve your results, look for help along the way, and don't give up—you will get there.

IT'S ABOUT TIME: RUN WITH, NOT AGAINST, THE CLOCK

"All we have to decide is what to do with the time that is given us."
—J.R.R Tolkien

Time. There never seems to be enough of it! Sometimes it crawls so slowly you can't imagine enduring one more minute; sometimes it races by so quickly you don't know where it went. Sometimes you are aware of every passing second; sometimes you lose track of it entirely. But one thing is certain: Once it has passed, time is not something you can recapture.

Because time is finite, it isn't a matter of whether there is or is not enough of it, but rather how you choose to spend it. Learning how to effectively manage your time is a habit that can set you up for success and reduce stress, both in college and beyond.

Learn to Master Time, or it Will Master You

It has been said that "There is never enough time to do everything, but there is always enough time to do the most important thing." The first step toward mastering your time is to look closely and clearly at how you are using it and whether you are allocating it to your most important thing.

CHALLENGE # 13: TRAPPING TIME THIEVES

Take a week, or if you can't take a full week, take at least three days, and journal how you use your time. Become obsessed about tracking every single thing. How long does it take to complete your morning routine: brushing your teeth, showering, getting dressed? How long do you spend on video games or watching Netflix? How much time do you spend on exercise, socializing, and sleep? Track everything: how long it takes you to run errands, do chores, commute to class, or work—whatever you do and however you spend your time.

Maybe most importantly of all, monitor and mark down all of the time you spend on social media. Before you start: Take a guess about how much time you spend across all social platforms. Next, note down every time you check your notifications, no matter how quick the interruption. You will be amazed at how time is siphoned away from your day when you aggregate all of the mini-distractions. Most people have no idea how much time they lose; even when they guess that they spend one to two hours, they almost always underestimate the time they really spend.

Learn to take charge of your time, because tasks will expand to fill however much time you allot for them. Before you start your task, think about how much time you expect it to take, how valuable it is, and how you plan to approach it. Put your biggest effort on your biggest priorities—not what feels urgent in the immediate moment, but where you will receive the most value in the long run. Eliminate as many distractions as you can, set your timer, and get to work! If your timer goes off before you are finished, take an assessment and decide whether to allot more time now (and if so, how much), or whether to allocate time later (and if so, when and how much).

The Myth of the Multi-Tasker

> *"You can do two things at once, but you can't focus effectively on two things at once."*
> —Gary Keller

You've heard the term, and maybe even thought it of yourself: "I'm great at multi-tasking." Multi-tasking is the attempt to do more than one thing at the same time. Unfortunately, multi-tasking is a myth. Human beings cannot focus on two tasks simultaneously. We're simply not wired that way. So when you try to do two (or more) things at once, like listening to a lecture and checking your social media notifications, for example, what you are really doing is switching your focus from one thing to another. Maybe really really quickly, at lightning speed, but switching nonetheless.

You may think that this task switching makes you productive, but in reality, it may be exacting a price that you don't see. First, switching between simultaneous tasks takes a lot of brain power. Each time you change your focus, you force your brain to interrupt your current thought, remember where you were with the other thought, and back and forth. The attempt to accomplish more, quickly, actually slows you down. Because it takes mental effort to switch between tasks, so-called "multi-tasking" disturbs your ability to get work done efficiently and effectively. It takes longer and is more difficult to complete two tasks at the same time, even something as simple as checking your notifications, than if you had focused on completing each task individually.

If you've been thinking that you've been multi-tasking so long that you feel you've developed it as a skill, you aren't alone. But studies have shown that people's perception of their effectiveness while multi-tasking strongly overestimates their actual effectiveness in performance. We think that we are more adept than we are when juggling between two tasks.

Furthermore, when you pull focus from one task and switch your attention away, you aren't aware of what you miss. That key sentence in the class lecture is lost while you are focusing on that email message. Or planning your next club meeting. Or writing your paper in your head.

Your depth of understanding of your course material is diminished when, instead of giving your full focus and attention to the passage you are reading, you are distracted by and engaging in a conversation with your roommate. You make more mistakes as your brain tries to quickly switch between separate tasks. And there can be a lag between when you think you've switched to a new task, but your brain is still thinking about the previous one.

Use Focus as a Force Multiplier

Since multi-tasking is a myth, and task switching is not ideal, an obvious step to increase your success is to focus your full attention and energy on one task at a time. This may be easier said than done, as you may need to break some bad habits. But once you've changed your approach to one of conscious single-tasking, you will be amazed at the benefits you'll obtain!

Make the decision to go to class or study WITHOUT your notifications on or communication apps open. Reserve specific times during your day to check messages; for example, allot fifteen minutes during your morning routine, another fifteen minutes at lunch, thirty minutes before or after dinner, and fifteen minutes after two hours of studying. Experiment with time blocks that work best for your concentration, perhaps short thirty-minute bursts with five-minute breaks to stay in the zone long-term, or a solid ninety minutes to really immerse yourself and complete key elements of your assignments, with a thirty-minute break to relax and recover. Use whatever works best with your ability to concentrate, stay motivated, and get results. Then set up your system to protect your flow.

Use "do not disturb" features on your cellphone and computer (and even your doorknob) to protect your focus time. Let your friends and family know when you will be available to hang out or catch up, and then don't respond to interruptions outside of those parameters. The point is to reduce distractions to enable you to focus and be comfortable in the knowledge that you won't miss anything important.

The Magical Power of No

Have you ever had that sinking feeling when someone asks you to do something that you really don't want to do? Whether the request is to join an activity, go to an event, or volunteer to help, family, church, social, or other "obligations"' can fill up your time and sap your energy if they aren't aligned with your goals. We often accept invitations because we feel we "have to." We worry that we will let someone down. But here's the thing: You don't have to say yes just because someone asks. Your time and energy are finite and you are the ultimate arbiter on how you spend them. You can choose.

Start with YOUR goals and plans, and make sure that you have those covered. Weigh the time and energy you have left against the choices you have left. Think about those activities that fill you up: your spirit, your physical and emotional balance, and give you joy. Consider whether your participation will be fun, give you a break, fulfill your desire to give back, or expand your knowledge.

Do you dread going to that party, feel weighed down by the demands of the club, worry about the time sink of participating in that event? Are you conflicted because you'd like to help lead that study group, but really need to focus on another class? If so, then just say no. "No, not this time." "No, I'm already committed." "Thank you for thinking of me, but no." Practice saying it gracefully, and stick to your guns. No guilt allowed! You have your own path and calling, and you need to keep your resources to fulfill that path. There will be other opportunities to say yes. The momentary disappointment and guilt you may feel will give way to joy as you free yourself to progress along your path.

Persistence Paves the Way

Not everything is going to go your way all the time and you may not immediately excel at every subject. Here's the part where you get to practice perseverance—another life skill that will serve you long after you graduate. Plenty of people have determination at the outset, when things are new and untested. But not everyone has the will to keep going when the going gets tough, or monotonous, or boring. The ability to grind it out, to keep putting in your best efforts even when your interest and passion fades, is critical. Companies pay college graduates higher salaries not just for the vocational training you gain, but because by making it to graduation, you have proven that you can stick it out through challenges and see your plan to completion. Stay the course. Finish the work. Anyone can do it, but not everyone does. So hang in there and remember your "why." Your persistence will be rewarded.

FINDING YOUR MO'(MENTUM) WHEN YOU DON'T KNOW OR DON'T WANT TO GO

"You gotta make it a priority to make your priorities a priority."
—Richie Norton

Here are some tips to trick your inner procrastinator and other ways to get unstuck:

- Physiology trumps psychology. If you are in a mental fog or slump, or just don't have any energy, vigorous physical activity can reinvigorate you. Put on some heart-pounding music and dance, do jumping jacks, take a brisk walk, make yourself move it, move it. Once your blood gets pumping, you'll be able to reclaim your mental focus and get going.

- Manage your mindset and train your brain to take the leap anyway. Motivational speaker Tony Robbins practices this through what he calls "priming." He starts every day with a two-minute cold plunge or shower. Unpleasant, yes, but it wakes up the nerves and gets the body ready to take action. When asked what he does on those mornings that he just doesn't feel like doing it, he says that he made the decision to adopt this habit and that he simply will not negotiate with himself. So once you have decided on your plan of action, don't allow temptation to sabotage the commitment you made to yourself. Take the action. Don't think about it. Just do it.

- Sometimes the biggest obstacle is just to start. Once you get going, it is easier to keep on going. So find the way to get that initial push.

Whether it is by creating energy through a brief workout, or taking a cold shower, or whatever method works for you, find a way to blast out of your current doldrums and make a start. Even a small step can get you going. Use momentum to create inertia in your favor. If you are finding the first step too daunting, consider another, efficient approach to the task. Or create a smaller step forward that you CAN take. Then take it right away. Sometime it's easier to stay in motion, and course correct if necessary, than to get in motion in the first place.

If you are procrastinating on the critical things, what are the things you did instead? Did they move you toward your goals? If not, and you simply can't get moving on one project, use your distraction to take action and make positive progress on another project. Make progress on your to-do's and let the momentum of that progress help you make your "TA-DA"s!

Conclusion

Remember Andrew? At the end of the semester, he looked back with satisfaction. More than the great grades he had achieved, his friendship with Olivia had opened the door to new friendships. The success of her study group had pulled in more people, including his roommate Jackson, who had been unpleasantly surprised with his first mid-term grades and needed to buckle down. Andrew's learning challenges caused him to have great study skills, and he became known in his dorm and beyond for helping people their overcome. When the dorm opened applications for Resident Advisors, many of his peers, now friends, insisted that Andrew apply.

It's on you to create the right learning environment for yourself, to build habits to support your goals, and to set yourself up for success. Do the hard work to make it easy to achieve your goals. Leverage the resources you have available to you. Use your time consciously. Make consistent forward progress and you will get there!

 **KEY TIPS**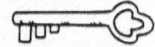

- KEEP SCORE! MAKE SURE THE EFFORTS YOU EXPEND PRODUCE THE RESULTS YOU WANT TO ACHIEVE. IF THEY DON'T, CHANGE YOUR PROCESS, APPROACH, OR HABITS TO IMPROVE YOUR EFFICIENCY.

- SCHEDULE YOUR CLASS ASSIGNMENTS, MAJOR PROJECTS, AND TESTS ONTO YOUR CALENDAR FROM EACH CLASS SYLLABUS. THEN BLOCK OUT TIME TO MAKE PROGRESS ON EACH ONE DAILY OR WEEKLY. BREAK YOUR WORK INTO SMALLER PIECES OR STEPS, SETTING SMART GOALS TO PROMOTE YOUR PROGRESS.

- TRACK HOW YOU USE YOUR TIME. REDUCE OR ELIMINATE TIME WASTERS, ENHANCE YOUR EFFICIENCY WHERE YOU CAN, AND TAKE CONTROL OF THE CLOCK.

Chapter 7

NAVIGATING YOUR SETBACKS

"Hardships often prepare people for an extraordinary Destiny."
—C.S. Lewis

Michiko has always had a bit of a love-hate relationship with public speaking. On the one hand, she had no problem sharing her, shall we say, advice? Opinions? Of which she had many, strongly held and fervently expressed, with no hesitation whatsoever.

On the other hand, Michiko also had an unfortunate habit of hyperventilating when speaking before a live audience. No matter how confident she feels going in, she develops the rapid shallow breathing, the flop sweat, and the overwhelming feeling that sometimes results in her locking her knees and fainting. Yes, full on, worry about how to fall without flashing the audience in her skirt, thumping to the floor, fainting. After each public speech, her fear of public speaking grew.

Now Michiko is in college, waiting to go onstage to give her group's presentation to the roughly 120 students in her European History class. Yes, she drew the short straw and was elected by her team to present for them, and no, they were completely unmoved by her desperate pleas concerning her past, um, performance problems.

So, onstage she went. And sure enough: About two minutes into the presentation, Michiko started hyperventilating, and down she went. She came to immediately on the ground, with a crowd surrounding her, wishing she was anywhere but there.....

Not every adventure goes exactly the way we plan it...

Failure is part of the journey. Whatever your mistakes, learn from them, grow, and use the lessons to fuel your future success. Learning can be a bit messy. Find joy in the perfect imperfect: Laugh at yourself, find the deeper meaning, and always cheer your own progress.

If you aren't failing at all, maybe you are playing it too safely and aren't challenging yourself enough. Remember that strength and next-level growth comes from pushing yourself to take on new and deeper challenges.

Confidence comes from going all in, playing full out, and achieving things that you didn't think you could. Resilience comes from knowing that you can survive, pick yourself up, and try again after you stumble. Both are key traits to learn on your college adventure and will serve you well throughout your life.

So what can you do to prepare for the pitfalls? Anticipate what you can, and pre-plan your disaster response.

CHALLENGE # 14: PRE-PLAN YOUR RECIPES FOR RECOVERY

Although it is true that you don't know what you don't know, you CAN imagine potential problems and pre-plan how you could address them. Think of it like preparing for a disaster and packing a doomsday pack with a flashlight, batteries, water bottles, granola bars; plotting your exit strategy in the event of a fire; determining where you will meet up with your family if you are separated.

In a similar way, you can plan ahead for potential catastrophes in college and create your own recipe for recovery. Having the tools and plan in place can help you lessen the impact, and maybe even avert the disaster altogether.

In this case, start by imagining what could go wrong. For example:

- Your internet connection fails when you need to submit a key assignment. Do you have places scoped out that provide free internet access—the library? A local coffee shop? Another dorm?

- Your professor is terrible as a teacher. Can you change classes? Is there another professor that teaches the class at a time that works with your schedule? Can you take it over the summer? What will be your plan if you absolutely must take the class from him? Can you form a study group to teach each other the material?

- Your computer crashes. Can you set things up in advance to back up your work at regular intervals? Do you have a habit of saving as you work on big projects or assignments? If you haven't set duplication in advance, do you have resources that can help you try to recover your work? Are there classes or other arenas where you want or need contact information? Do you have your insurance information, family contact information, or other key information collected in an accessible place or with another trusted friend?

Take time to imagine as many ways as you can that things could go wrong, and for each one, think about and create a response plan that includes what you can do to prepare in advance and what you would do to recover.

Sometimes your recipe may include having backup batteries or other materials. Sometimes it may call for setting up your computer to make automatic saves on your projects. Other circumstances may call for having a phone tree or contact information for a member of your class. Consider things that you can do BEFORE the problem occurs to minimize its impact.

Now take it to the next level: plan what you would do if you haven't acted in advance or an unanticipated crisis arises. Plan how you can approach the problem when need a response to an emergency in the moment.

Having these plans in place can help you in two ways: First, you will be prepared for those things that you anticipate; second, you will have gained some experience in thinking through challenging circumstances, which may help you as you react to unforeseen crises.

The more and better you prepare yourself mentally, the better off you will be. And if you take action to prepare in advance, you'll be better still.

WHEN YOU HIT A PERSONAL POTHOLE AND YOUR ADVENTURE VEERS OFF-TRACK

"Tough times don't last, tough people do."
—Robert Scholler

It may sound glib, but it's true: If there is no struggle, there is no progress. In college, you will be called on to push beyond your comfort zone and current strengths. You will face obstacles, failures, and falls along your journey. So prepare yourself—get comfortable with this reality and get back on the horse! Assess the damage, learn from your lumps, and action ahead.

Look at failure the way Thomas Edison did: Every time you don't succeed, you've eliminated another route that prevents you from succeeding. There is very little from which you irrevocably can't recover if you resolve to recommit to your dream, learn from your mistakes, create new goals, schedule success, and take corrective action.

Don't Panic—Plan It!

Earlier chapters discussed how to use your calendar/planner to allocate your time and how to use your syllabus to map out time to complete assignments and longer-term projects. But sometimes those plans can slip—finishing your assignments can take longer than expected, or perhaps a new assignment pops up that throws off your plan.

There will be times, especially at the end of semesters, when it seems like all of your projects, papers, and tests converge and are all due at the same time. You know that panicky feeling when you have so many things to do that your mind jumps from one to the next and you can't work on anything without thoughts of the other things racing around in your head? Deadlines! No time! You feel like you've drunk ten cups of coffee: Your pulse rate is sky high, you can't focus, and you're beginning to think that you cannot possible survive this.

First of all—don't panic! You are not alone in this mess, but you alone can determine whether and how well you will make it out of it. Take a deep breath, or maybe ten. Calm your heart. And then take a few minutes to make a written list of exactly what you need to do and by when you need to complete each task. Break big tasks into a series of smaller steps (and remember your SMART goals from Chapter 6). Often when people panic, they feel as if they don't have time to put together a game plan. But taking a few minutes to create a game plan allows you to take the swirling thoughts out of your head and put them down on paper in a list.

This list will let you see exactly what you need to do and let you form a tactical plan to get it done. You can visualize the order that you will work on each item and allocate the amount of time you can spend on each one. It will help you create control out of chaos.

You Can't Boil the Ocean

Have you ever faced a challenge so big, so overwhelming, that you not only can't imagine getting it done, but you don't even know where to begin? There are a number of metaphors for that feeling: eating an elephant, boiling the ocean... basically, the idea is that you can't take on a project that big all at once. You need to break it down to smaller, more manageable steps. You take one step at a time to make progress toward your goal. If you begin the process with enough time, you will be able to finish your project, assignment, or preparation for that test, with minimal stress.

But what if you didn't plan well enough ahead and your projects all converge with due dates at the same time?

Invest Your Time to Maximize Returns

One approach when you're facing a time crunch is to optimize the use of the time you do have. If you don't have enough time fully to accomplish all of your projects, look at the weighted value of each project you have to do. Then prioritize those activities that have the highest value. For example, if the value of the paper is thirty percent of your grade, the homework assignment one percent, and the quiz five percent, you will want to devote most of the time to your paper. Know yourself and how you work best—if knocking off the items that are easiest to do will help you concentrate, plan to do that, but make sure that you have a strict time limit on the how much time you will allow yourself to spend to get the small projects done.

Use the weight of each task to guide the effort you expend on it, as well. If you are crunched for time and know that homework is only one percent of your grade, merely turning the work in on time is sufficient. If instead this particular homework assignment is fifty percent of your grade, you will want to allocate time and spend a lot more energy to do the best job possible.

Most people automatically work on those assignments that are easiest for them to do, not necessarily those that yield the highest return for them (i.e. mean the most for their grades). But by making a conscious effort to spend your time on the activities that matter most, you will maximize the results of your work within the time you have.

In situations where perfection just isn't possible, know that you are doing your best and okay is good enough. For the larger or more important projects, use your time and energy where it will make the most difference.

And then learn the lesson from this experience: Look ahead to future projects and plan how to not get yourself in this type of time crunch in the future. Even if it worked out this time, do you really want the unnecessary stress and aggravation again?

Sometimes people procrastinate so that they don't have to risk trying hard and failing anyway. Learning to put out your best efforts bravely and consistently is an invaluable life skill and will make you stronger. Give yourself the chance to give your all, without the excuse that "it would have been better if I'd had more time."

CHANGE YOUR PERSPECTIVE; CHANGE YOUR WORLD

Tennis star Billie Jean King once said that "Pressure is a privilege— let it call forth your greatness." But she also noted that "pressure can crush you". The key is to know the difference, and to use the former but avoid the latter.

Did you ever see that commercial that mocks almost every scary movie ever made? The commercial has a group of scared teens trying to decide where to go to avoid the killer. They look over to an old barn that has chain saws and knives and scythes and other scary implements. The camera pans over to a running car. One of the teens says, "But why can't we just get in the car?" Instead they rush to the barn. The camera pans to the killer in the barn behind them, who rolls his eyes.

When you are panicked and feel out of control, you can't think clearly. You can miss the solution right in front of you. The more frantic you feel, the less rationally you can deal with the situation. Knowing this in advance, promise yourself that you will not make any major decisions or take any rash action while you are in this state.

If you can, step back to evaluate your circumstances. Is this a passing tempest? Or is this a real crisis? Both may feel the same in the moment, so be sure to ask an objective third party to help you navigate. Use a trusted friend (or two!) to help you regain your perspective. Check in with your network or college resources to assess whether you're seeing things clearly.

Don't let your insecurities drive you off your path. When you think that you can't, you won't. So take a moment to acknowledge your feelings, then put in place a plan to address them.

Take a break. Pull out the list of strengths that you packed and remind yourself of your superpowers. Remind yourself of your "why," and let that motivate you. Put on your power music and let that pump you up. Take a walk and let nature revitalize you. Allow yourself a few minutes to watch funny videos.

Change the channel. Take your mind out of your current worry and think about a broader view. Make a mental list of all of the things you are grateful for RIGHT NOW and keep at it until you really feel it. You can't be miserable in a state of gratitude. So count your blessings and think about all of the things you are thankful for. If you can change your attitude, you can change everything. No matter how dire your difficulties are in any given moment, I guarantee that there is someone somewhere who has it worse.

You may be thinking, "So what? I'm miserable and it will NEVER be better." That is up to you, and you need to take charge. Seek out help if you need it—colleges have resources dedicated to psychological and emotional health. These resources are there for you, so use them to help. They can help you work through your troubles and deal with your feelings. Emotions can be more fleeting than you think. They can change in an instant. If you can just hang in there, this (whatever it is) will pass. Learn to recognize, acknowledge, and master your feelings, and you can survive the storm and create an experience as awesome as you want it to be.

Shame in the Shadows, Sunlight as Disinfectant

Matt just graduated from Stanford—*thirty years* after he first started college. He had partied too hard, slept through classes, and failed too many courses to graduate with his class. So he dropped out, became an alcoholic, and carried the shame of his failure for decades until he decided to finish his remaining courses and obtain his degree. In the interim, he got his drinking under control, had a successful career, and married and raised a family. So the degree itself was, on one level, unimportant. But his failure to graduate was a stone in his shoe, a failure that he carried in secret, until he finally decided to do something about it. He did finish his courses, he did get his degree, and he wrote an article about his experience in an alumni magazine.

Matt said that he had been hesitant to write the article. Ashamed of his past, he felt vulnerable exposing it. Especially to this community. But after the article came out, Matt was amazed at the responses. People came out of the woodwork praising him for his honesty, many saying they shared his challenges. They were inspired by his courage to face his fears and follow through on his commitments to himself. In the end, Matt said that his biggest regret was that he carried his secret for so long, and lost the opportunity to help others learn from his experience earlier.

Here's the thing: It's really easy to think that everyone else has it easy. But it just isn't true. We each of us have our own challenges and burdens. We ALL make mistakes and have things that we might do differently if we had the chance. But life moves only in one direction—forward—so the only choice we have is how we want to proceed. Take your lumps, learn your lessons, then move on.

Think about who you admire. My guess is they've had plenty of challenges to overcome. That's part of what makes them so inspiring. Be compassionate with yourself and decide to be, or do, better. Rather than hold onto embarrassment, shame, or regret, why not try to turn your experience into something that can help someone else? Sharing the perils you've encountered on your personal journey may save someone else pain. It may help you refine your thinking on the experience. It may lessen your burden. And the positive response you get may surprise you.

The other thing to consider is what "never giving up" means to you. It may be turn out that, despite your best plans, your journey doesn't unfold as you planned it. If you are persistent, resilient, and use the resources available to you, you can figure out a way forward out of almost any mess.

 **WHAT TO DO WHEN YOU'RE BLUE**

When you're down, and there will be times that you will be, here are five tips and tricks to help you weather the storm. Know upfront that there will be stormy seas, setbacks, and blunders, and prepare yourself in advance to make it through to the other side:

1. **I can see clearly now the rain has gone: Prospecting your perspective.** You've heard the saying, "This too shall pass." And you've no doubt had trauma and drama in your past that felt like the world was ending in the moment. But notice how it feels much less momentous with a little time and distance. The same will be true with whatever challenges you're facing now. Visualize yourself after this challenge as a means to motivate yourself through it.

2. **Filter your focus to f-stop your feelings: Diminish depression using perspective.** There are ALWAYS people who are much worse off than you. Shift your focus to the many blessings you have and find a way to be of service to others who are less fortunate. Many colleges have community service projects that you can volunteer with. Giving back feels good and makes a difference to people in need. Helping others truly will help yourself out of your slump.

3. **Challenge yourself to change your mind(set) radically: what's great about this?** There are always lessons to learn, even, and sometimes especially, in the most challenging times. Take a break and do something that will bring you joy, and use the opportunity to change your perspective. Think about what this experience has done <u>for you</u>, in a positive way. Remember your underdog advantages, and consider whether this, too, can be recast as a strength.

4. **Use music (and move) to make your mood.** Use the playlist you already set up (or, if you haven't got one yet, set it up now and use it) to fuel your fighter, and uplift your spirits. Use the soundtracks to get you moving. Take a brisk walk or run, go for a swim. Use physical activity to bleed off your anxiety, reduce your depression, and change your mood.

5. **Engage the power of the collective**: No one has to go it alone. Make a positive choice not to suffer in silence. Even if you don't want to share your struggles with a trusted friend, your peers, or your family, there is support for you. Your college will have resources to help you sort through your blues—engage them! Having a third party to bounce ideas off of, or to share your burdens, to hear your concerns and to brainstorm solutions is a superpower that you always have in your back pocket. You don't have to take their advice if you don't want to. But why not use them as a sounding board to help you through? You will feel better if you do, and they will feel better for having helped.

Cheaters Never Prosper, They Only Cheat Themselves

Please, please, please don't make this mistake. If you get in a time crunch and aren't prepared, you can try to see if you can get an extension on the deadline for the paper or the test. Obviously, the earlier you ask for this, the better, and there is no guarantee that you will get one.

If you don't, and your only choice is to cheat or to fail—fail. It is much easier to recover from that experience than it is to recover from getting caught cheating, or cheating yourself even if you don't get caught. And don't fool yourself: Colleges know all about the online resources where you pay to have someone write that paper for you. And they've seen the pre-written papers for sale before too. Just don't do it.

A SHARED JOURNEY LIFTS ALL

We humans are not meant to live in isolation. Whether you are an introvert or extrovert, you are not a solitary being. Don't allow yourself to disconnect from your fellow students. Be sure actively to build relationships with those around you. It will bolster you when you feel alone and will offer you the opportunity to be there for someone when they are in need.

If you feel lost, alone, or vulnerable, reach out. It's NEVER as bad as it seems, and a friend, colleague, mentor, tutor, professor, or administrator can be just the ticket to give you the perspective you need to weather your personal storm.

While you're at it, consider this: You may not be able to control how well you did on that last test, your irritation with your roommate, or your embarrassment at not having an answer when called on in your seminar. But you can control how you show up in the world. You can smile at a fellow student. You can compliment someone on a good point they made in class. Buy a coffee for the person behind you in line. Spread some kindness. You never know what that small gesture may mean to someone else and what good they, in turn, may be inclined to do as a result. Your action starts a ripple in the pond that goes beyond what you may see.

Our lives are enhanced by our shared experiences. Share your joys and sorrows, and you will enrich your experience and that of those around you.

NAVIGATING SETBACKS

Here are some essential things to remember when you hit potholes on your journey:

- **Your Thoughts Shape Your Life.** Everything starts with a thought, which impacts your feelings, actions, and ultimately, your results. If you're not happy with the results in your life, you have the power to change everything, starting with changing your thoughts.

- **What's done is done.** Don't dwell on the past. It's quite literally the ONE thing you CAN'T change. Focus instead on what you CAN change and what you're going to do TODAY to have a better tomorrow.

- **Worrying is a waste of time and emotion.** Worrying accomplishes nothing, yet we all do it, sometimes seemingly constantly. Learn to acknowledge that you're worried, and then intentionally put it away. Learning to let go of this emotion will make your experience easier.

- **Addition by subtraction.** Be mindful of the people you surround yourself with. Keep your distance from people who bring you down, suck energy out of you, or make you feel bad. Those people don't deserve your time or energy; subtract the time and energy you spend on them. Save it for those who lift you up... and lift them up too.

- **Enjoy the ride.** Once you get to a milestone, another one appears... and then another... and another. We tend to keep moving our eyes forward, never fully allowing ourselves to enjoy the process and celebrate key victories along the way. Enjoy the ride and don't forget that there's growth and value for you to mine in the process.

Conclusion

Remember Michiko? Luckily, the professor didn't allow cellphones in class, so no one made a video of her fainting—thank goodness! But word still spread across campus and well beyond her class. She was often greeted with, "Hey, fainting girl" as she walked to class, to school clubs, to parties.

Embarrassing? Yes. Humiliating in the moment? Sure. Life destroying? No. Not really. Over time, Michiko was able to find the humor and laugh at the incident along with everyone else. She took some meditation and breathing classes to help her get over her stage fright, and with practice, she learned to manage her fears when she had to do public speaking.

And she met people that she otherwise might not have, people who were not intimidated to start a conversation with someone so clearly less than perfect. She made some friends that she'll have for life (and who will never let her forget her mishap; always good for a laugh, they think). She came to realize that everyone has flaws and insecurities, and that's what makes us all authentically human.

So as you travel through your college adventure, have a sense of humor, and take your lumps and learnings with grace. Good things can come out of bad experiences. The connections you make will make your experience awesome and may last your whole life.

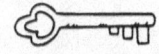 **KEY TIPS**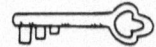

- YOU WILL INEVITABLY HIT OBSTACLES AND SUFFER SETBACKS ON YOUR JOURNEY. HOW YOU PREPARE FOR THEM, AND RESPOND TO THEM, WILL DEFINE YOUR OUTCOME.

- PERSPECTIVE AND PROPER SUPPORT CAN GUIDE YOU THROUGH ADVERSITY. BE YOUR OWN BEST ADVOCATE.

- LESSONS AREN'T ALWAYS EASILY LEARNED OR PAINLESS, BUT IF YOU SHARE YOUR EXPERIENCES, YOU CAN HELP YOURSELF AND OTHERS TOO, WHICH CAN REDUCE THE STING OF THE FALL.

Conclusion

*"Today you are YOU. That is truer than true.
There is no one alive who is You-er than You."*

—Dr. Seuss

Yes, your college adventure will be filled with new challenges. Some may be fearsome, adrenalin-boosting, heart-racing experiences. Some will have steep learning curves and happen at a speed beyond your current capabilities. You will have opportunities to stumble, and flail, and fall. But with the right mindset, habits, and tools, you will be able to gain the knowledge, experience, and skills that will serve you the rest of your life. If you follow the steps in this guide, you will be able not just to survive, but to thrive in college.

Three years after graduation, a group of college friends met up for Homecoming weekend. Pete flew in from New York. The focus he gained freshman year from the Rex debacle helped him build the skills he was using at his investment bank. Maria had stayed local; after all her moves before college, she was happy to have found her home at the school and now works as the college liaison with the Alumni Association. Susannah merged her many interests and works promoting global recycling initiatives for an NGO (non-government organization) based out of Washington, D.C. Jean-Carlos discovered his love of travel and works in international sales for a tech company headquartered in Austin. Michiko is working part-time in a medical clinic while she is applying to medical schools. Tyrone took his coding expertise and joined a software company that creates gaming apps in San Francisco. Andrew uses his organizational skills to help Jackson launch his film production company in Atlanta and keep it on track; they have a documentary that has generated industry buzz and may get them an Oscar nomination. Olivia went immediately to law school in Chicago and is set to graduate this year.

The friends all laughed and reminisced about their college days. In retrospect, the stress, lack of sleep, uncertainty, and challenges they encountered in their college journey made them all stronger and more confident in facing their current challenges. Some noticed that they had learned lessons beyond their classes that prepared them for life in ways they hadn't expected, or even realized at the time.

They talked about what they were currently doing, their triumphs and trials, and, just like old times, they offered each other suggestions and support. They left after the weekend with a promise to keep in touch more often (which some kept better than others), but knowing that they had friends for life.

You, too, can make it through your college adventure successfully—and you will surely collect plenty of stories along the way.

You might be feeling excitement, nervousness, or even overwhelming anxiety. This is totally normal when you step outside your comfort zones and take on new challenges. You may feel it at the start of your college journey and you may feel it again at graduation as you prepare to take the next step on your life journey. You are not alone.

But you ARE alone in taking charge of your adventure. You can conquer new challenges if you set your goals, face your fears, push past doubts, prepare yourself, take action, and let yourself fly! This is your life, and it is all up to you. Choose to make it awesome!

And in the end, this isn't the end, it is just the beginning...

Index of Challenges

OFFER TO READERS

Do you have any stories of how you used the tips and tricks in this book? Want to share what worked for you, what didn't, what you learned, and what you know now that you wished you had known then? I'd love to hear from you!

And if you would like to have the chance to have your story included in the author's next book: "CRUSHING IT IN COLLEGE: AVOIDING PITFALLS AND POTHOLES ON THE ROAD TO SUCCESS IN COLLEGE AND LIFE," send your feedback and learn more on my website at www.aliciajmoore.com.

Acknowledgements

It takes a village to raise … a book. In my case I have so many people to thank, I can only list a few of those without whom this wouldn't have been possible:

First, Dean Graziosi, whose teaching made me take action. His thoughts about deep motivation and practical use of knowledge are transformational.

Geoffrey Berwind, master storyteller, Verdi lover and essential histories archaeologist, who helped me mine my personal truths. Sarah Brown, Cristina Smith, Amy Reed and Dawn Rafferty all provided critical insights and guidance, for which I am deeply grateful.

Bob Harpole, who went above and beyond to keep me on task and on track. You made my journey enjoyable at every step. Rob, Steve, Meghan, Liz and the BSP team, you all rock!

Anne Bonfiglio, who graciously agreed to tackle the alpha version and helped me hack through the jungle.

James Seifert, who suffered through the alpha AND beta versions, and whose thoughtful comments vastly improved everything. You enhance my life in ways too profound to express. Thank you!

Will Seifert, who has proven that the steps in this guide can work for anyone willing to put in the effort. Congratulations on your selection to the Dean's List in all semesters, and for always being the inspirational and compassionate man you are.

Lauren Taylor, an amazing teacher and friend. Your contributions and wisdom were invaluable. Amanda Sorensen, who captured my vision in the interior graphics.

To my many high school and college interviewees and beta readers who were so generous in sharing their thoughts, concerns, and experiences. I won't embarrass you by calling you out by name, but you know who you are. To the extent that this guide is valuable to incoming college students, it will be largely because of your generous participation.

To my husband, Mike, who watched with incredulity as I finally pushed through to make this dream a reality. You are my rock and roll, hoochie koo.

And finally, to my readers! Thank you for giving me your time and attention. I hope that you find value in the tips and tricks, and use them to set yourself up not just to survive, but to thrive, on your college adventure. Wishing you happy, healthy, and fulfilling lives in which this journey is just the beginning!

About The Author

With degrees and certificates from Stanford University, UCLA School of Law, and the Haas School of Business at UCBerkeley, respectively, Alicia continues to crush it in college. Alicia is the CEO of Strategic Impact Solutions. She serves as a member of the Board of Directors for the innovative Bay Area Resource Area for Teachers (RAFT), an educational nonprofit that supports teachers and promotes STEAM and kinesthetic learning.

As a senior executive in pre-money, private start-up through $1B+ public companies, Alicia built, bought, integrated and ran legal, HR, corporate business personal and professional development, and administration departments. She is well known for helping individuals, teams, groups, companies, and Boards of Directors create and successfully achieve strategic, tactical and developmental goals.

Alicia is passionate about the value of life-long education as a foundation to create transformative growth. Her series of workshops and online courses support her mission to spread the joy of learning to everyone, regardless of age and background. She has spoken as a keynote and on panels at several events, and provides consulting services by engagement.

When she isn't working with people on their growth goals, you can find Alicia hanging out with her family and friends, traveling the world, attending sporting events, and—you guessed it—learning new things.

Please visit the author's website at www.aliciajmoore.com for more information and opportunities to work with Alicia.